Combinations | OF THE | Universe

Combinations

OF THE | *Universe*

ALBERT GOLDBARTH

The Ohio State University Press | Columbus

Library of Congress Cataloguing-in-Publication Data

Goldbarth, Albert.
    Combinations of the universe : poems / Albert Goldbarth.
        p. cm.
    ISBN 0-8142-0925-4 (alk. paper) — ISBN 0-8142-5105-6 (pbk. : alk. paper) —
    ISBN 0-8142-9001-9 (CD Rom)
    I. Title
    PS3557.O354 C565 2003
    811'.54—dc21

                                                    2002013169

Cover by Dan O'Dair.
Type set in Electra.
Printed by Thomson-Shore.

The paper used in this publication meets the minimum requirement of the American
National Standard for Information Sciences—Permanence of Paper for Printed Library
Materials.
ANSI Z39.48-1992

9 8 7 6 5 4 3 2 1

"The Omnipresent," said a Rabbi, "is occupied in making marriages." The levity of the saying lies in the ear of him who hears it; for by marriages the speaker meant all the wondrous combinations of the universe whose issue makes our good and evil.

—GEORGE ELIOT

The universe, in Judaeo-Christian tradition, is conceived of as a written Book made from numbers and letters; the key to understanding the universe lies in our ability to read these properly and master their combination.

—ALBERTO MANGUEL

CONTENTS

ACKNOWLEDGMENTS

Another Chicago Magazine: NaCl; Repositories

Antioch Review: The Gold Star (also reprinted in *The Best American Poetry 2002*)

Bellingham Review: The Branch; How I Want to Go; Stonehenge; Too Much Use

Beloit Poetry Journal: The Girl Who Married a Wooden Pounder

Boulevard: Getting to See; The Gunshot in the Parking Lot:; A *Woman Bathing in a Stream*, 1654

Columbia: One of Them Speaks:

Georgia Review: Jan. 31st: Degrees of the Same Thing; Some Cloths; "The Burden of Modernity": The Book, the God, the Child (also reprinted in *Georgia Review* Poetry Chapbook Series #3); Eye of Beholder; Moonology; Alteration; Fahrenheit 451

Gettysburg Review: Futures; Ham(s); On the Beach with the Vikings; Rock; The Song of the Tags; The Words "Again" and "Groovy"

Green Mountains Review: The S.D.G.I.E.

Hampden-Sydney Poetry Review: Call 1-800-THE-LOST

Iowa Review: Apology; Laws of the Universe; The Song of Too Much

Kenyon Review: The Splinter Groups of Breakfast

Laurel Review: The Book of Human Anomalies; The Sonnet for Planet 10; "We call it birth . . ."; Cord

Mid-American Review: Mouth; Vessels

New England Review: A Yield

Ohio Review: The Polarized Responses

Ontario Review: Far; Some Deaths That Have Recently Come to My Attention

Pleiades: In One Night

Poetry: The Bar Cliché; Maypurés; Past Presidents of the Counters Club; Stationed; Zero: Terror / Lullabye; Inside

Poetry East: "I remember, from my childhood . . ."; The Lives of the Artists; Packing for a Difficult Trip

Poetry International: D___ L ___'s

Prairie Schooner: The Sequel to "The Sonnet for Planet 10"

Quarterly West: The Cosmology of Empty; From the Moon; Hierarchy, Lowerarchy

Salt Hill: Civilized Life; The Waltzers
Seneca Review: Drugstore, 1958
Shenandoah: Myth Studies
Southwest Review: This Cartography
TriQuarterly: Jodi
Western Humanities Review: Remains Song
Willow Springs: Some Secret

"Apology," "Laws of the Universe," and "The Song of Too Much" were part of a
group of poems that received the *Iowa Review*'s 2001 Tim McGinnis Award:
thanks to David Hamilton.

Jan. 31st: Degrees of the Same Thing

The astrophysicist said

that what we are is walking carbon—that we're carbon, on loan from the hearts of the stars, and if she thought that anyone in her youngish audience even vaguely knew what "carbon paper" was, she'd make a little joke on "carbon copies," which is what we are, but they didn't, although they knew silicon, as in chips, and it was true there too: the spectrum-mark for silicon, first seen inside the stellar light in the pioneering work of the 1920s, is inarguably a "line match" with the spectrum-mark for the silicon underfoot in our home planet, as if—on the level of elements—Siamese twins were joined together not by gristle or ligament . . . but light-years. She reminded us: astronomy is also genealogy; that somewhere in between the first bacterium and stellar radiation is a family connection; that the sky is amniotic. And our lives, she said, respond to—are a part of—waves of quantum-level flux that fill—in some ways *are*—the universe. She told us a biologist would say the same: the crystals in the Earth; the crystal systems in our cells. As if there might be two tin cans from Periodic Table soup, and a connecting string ("Hello, is a human being there? *Hello?*") that lightly hummed, that made for a faint but viable line of communication.

The parapsychologist said

this might explain what "hunch" is; "inspiration"; "teleportation"; "ghosts"; "telepathy"; "out-of-the-body travel"; "holy visions"; "angels"; "demons"; "premonition"; "E.S.P." He said the voice that insinuated itself with the weight of a plumber's snake inside the ear canal of Joan of Arc might well be God, or one of God's bewingéd messengers, or we could say it might be the results of a bipolar reconstruction of the brain's synaptic patterns. Then again, it might more simply be the fabric of the universe conversing with its weave. The same with Abraham, when the air was alive with utterance and commanded him to go at the row of small clay infidel gods with a cudgel. The same with Ezekiel. William Blake, who hobnobbed over strong gray English tea with visiting seraphim. Your aunt, who woke at 3 A.M. from a dream of her sister's death—your mother—and then the phone confirmingly rang. We live inside great waves of electromagnetism; great waves of electromagnetism live inside *us*.

Every second, neutrinos are penetrating our flesh. The genes are issuing constant edicts. We couldn't *not* be awed receptors: "spirits"; "speaking in tongues"; "hallucinations"; "aliens"; "reincarnation." Every moment-"here" is also somewhere else's moment-"there." The curtains hang straight down. In drowned Atlantis, of course, they float upward.

My friend Janine said,

listen to me, in seventh-grade biology we kept a tadpole's heart alive in a tray of salt solution, and I saw that it was beating to match my own heart's rhythm, later I saw the pulsing of the stars *and it matched too*, and also "too" and "two" link up, so these make "two" too, so it's all dendritic connection, see? But *They* don't see, They give me paper cups of pills, They give me prefab batteries of tests about my nightmares, but They don't see how the six-point Star of David and the snowflake have a structural alliance, and since the David Star is still by definition *a star*, I've proved that it pulses along with my heart. You see that, right? That lightwaves *means* light-pulses. So then we know it's alive. It's all science: logic and proof. The light is alive; the angels aren't really Bible angels, they're ambassadors of light. I was a science major, Albert, did you know, it's why I see these things, and I'm afraid for the Earth right now, it's a message I have, we aren't paying attention enough to the living light, and two-eyes-two-ears-one-cunt-and-one-anal-hole is six, so we're a star of openings, all of us, but we're out of communication with the light and the snow and the other living beings, I'm here to give us hope, and all They do is sign me out of my room and sign me in again.

The sky said,

"it's your birthday," and it was—my fifty-fifth—and I walked out, and under its winter-sharpened pinpoint constellations, as I do each year on this day, to be alone with "my" celestial signs: a ritual made traditional by many years of annual repeating. Yes, but when I say "The sky said," I don't mean the sky *said anything*, not vocally: the phrase is a conventional poeticism, not the sign of an audibly rumbling confidence transmitted through the puzzle-part bones in the ear. Of course I do understand that we live in a web the size of space and time, and that its strands are always tugging at our minds (although it's also just as accurate to say its strands *comprise* our minds). And I've listened, I've set my head against the door—let's call it a "door"—of that vast otherness/allness/unknowableness surrounding us and in us. I've extended—let's say "hand"—my hand, and felt a power out there that can claim a life and scorch it to the root. And yet

I'm sane: I haven't listened until the voices finally made my skull their aviary; I've sensed the heat, but never set my hand flat on its surface. This has saved me, I suppose. Perhaps it's a failing as well; an unwillingness. It was my birthday, and I walked below the heavens, which I know are fraught with portent, even though they kept a distant, collegial silence with me; while somewhere, someone else was razor-whipped by the tails of comets into a splattered and jabbering thing, and someone else began to feel the unavoidable pull of the full moon on the protein infrastructure of the beast—its fangs, its bloodlust—that we normally keep well-hidden in us, and someone else encountered a spiral of sky on fire and felt it igniting his marrow, and painted its great fierce beauty, and sawed through his ear, and placed this on a plate for the sky to bend to, for the sky to pour itself into and burn, the sky to wander the maze of that ear with a piercing, intimate whisper.

Gods / Ancestors / Rituals

The Polarized Responses

1.

Of course the gods are alive! . . . they're *gods*.
These two, for instance: Siva
Vrsabhavahana, he of the svelte,
compactly muscled runner's body;
and Parvati, she of the tidy waist
and hips as richly packed as picnic baskets. They
attend to their celestial business: weather,
cycles, essence, fate. They powwow
with their sibling gods, or war
with them in competitions of miracles,
or lounge on beds of cloud. And with
an interest that's still loftily removed, they listen
every day to the wants of their human petitioners,
and indulge in the perk of a deity:
adoration. They get bathed
by the devoted in water of diamond and gold,
in sandal water, in water infused with plaska-fig,
acacia, ficus, banyan, and in cow milk,
curd, ghee, coconut milk, and honey,
and they're dressed in moons and flowers of gold,
in tigerskin and snakes, and they get serenaded
with Vedic hymns, and virgins dance before them,
and then, as the festival drums and finger-cymbals play,
they get paraded about the village in a temple-car
drawn either by bulls or by worshipers, and those
who come to view strew flowers upon their path.
—Unless they're on display
in a museum; then, they're art. They're bronze.
Inert. "Iconic housements of divinities."
No less a potent nexus of attention, necessarily; but
things that could be carried—there,
you see it? *things*—and stored in a vault
with other on-loan, high-insurance artifacts.

—And so the marriage. For him, it was an object now,
an image of a marriage, nothing more: the living marrow of it
slipped out long ago, and what was left
were two extraordinary dolls. But she
still rouged their cheeks, and laved them
with yolk and with musk and with sensual gels
that heat when breathed on, and she dressed them
in their silks, and she paraded them
through Mardi Gras, through New Year's Eve,
and they sang, and they waved to their mutual friends,
through years of anniversaries.

2.

—The polarized responses
Walter Benjamin calls "cult value"
versus "exhibition value." The tiger
is *vitally* alive to the seven-year-old boy
in the comic strip, it tussles, slurps, and romps,
though when the parents enter Thursday's
final panel, it's a stuffed toy
you could easily fit in a backpack.
Oh we live, oh we live, oh we live, oh we live
in a universe of vastly discrepant investitures;
this is our bounty *and* our woe.
Not that I mean to link the ethos
of "cult value" to a child's perceptions only;
in the adult novels of John Cowper Powys,
nothing is inanimate: each gatepost has its drowsy nerve
of philosophy, every stone in a roadside overgrowth of ratweed
is entitled to its crankiness, its mineral forgiveness.
In his *Atlantis*, we readers are privy to the thoughts
of the now-abandoned, fire-blackened, veteran
war club of the demigod Herakles; out of what serves
for mind in the grain of its wood, it offers on page 15
(of the first Macdonald & Company edition) its observation
on waking: "So I am still myself," it thinks
—if not profound, not different from what you or I
have noticed, with the same small disbelief, on the nearer side
of the great divide of eight hours of sleep.

Though, granted, animism is naturally more likely in
(and also cynically foisted upon) our childhoods:
the derby-sporting molar yodeling jingles
on behalf of toothpaste X; a rubber figure of that molar,
so continuously wished upon and handled,
we can understand how "doll" and "idol" have a common
/—*Albert, put your toys away, it's time*
to leave! I was six. My grandmother's funeral.
It turns out there are things the world won't breathe
the life back into, not the merest tinge of life,
not if you pray, you cry, you wake up wet
and screaming. She was there in her box,
as fakely rouged as a dime-store puppet.
Not if you said her name over and over.
Not if you called to her over and over.

3.

   This bone is alive,
the soul of an enemy warrior roils within it
like breath in a flute,
and so it's worn about the throat.
   This figurine of orthodontia wire,
orange rind, and the feathers of mountain thrushes
is a net for catching spirits, and they thrive there,
they inhabit the figurine.
   You see this baseball? Here: how perfect
in its roundness; even so, the stitching lets it understand
the needling pain that makes a human life;
and the calm at its center. . . . You can't tell *me*
that when I hear its thoughts it isn't Buddha.
   And I don't believe there's *one* of us who requires
astronomical proof that stars exist
in the "crazy bone" in the elbow.
They're inside, all right: constellated there,
and also strung in webs through the whole of our bodies.
The sky is a Mercator projection
of this, the sky is the outside indication
of that dazzle. And to this extent,
the sky is alive. There isn't an element in us

that it didn't have first, that it didn't *create*, in the time
when "alive" was fetally waiting
inside molecular bonding.
  Kere. Kesakten. And *tondi.* Or, more common
to the lexicon of Western thought because
of our oodles of studies of Melanasian custom,
mana . . . what Werner Muenstenberger calls
"intrinsic life-force, imported to various things
such as stones," which then become "organisms
permeated with basic strengths."
  Her toe shoes. That she practiced
her *en pointe* in, fourteen hours every day.
Here: where they're red
with her blood. This must have happened often enough
for us to call it transfusion.

  4.

A few times, when I was younger and could actually
be found at a synagogue service, I've lifted
the Torah, and—an honor—ceremonially
walked it about the room.
It's as heavy and large as the Word of God
should be, and the proper way to hold it is really
to cradle it, as if one arm is applying a tender pressure
around a partner's shoulders. Mostly,
though, you'll find that it's the eldest of the men
who undertake this honor; or probably,
these days, care at all. Very often
they're widowers. They have more room
for God by then. In any case, the Torah gets escorted
through the aisles in this pious
and physically intimate embrace
as, one by one, those in attendance kiss their prayer-shawl fringe,
then touch it to the Torah's sides: an act of vast devotion
to religious ideology, but scaled to a small
and domestic affection. And she's dressed
(because they sometimes do use "she," and *Jewish Ceremonial Art*
by Abram Kanof does say "dressed") in fitting splendor:
the mantle, of velvet or silk; the breastplate (*tas*)

of gold, with scarlet linen, and with twelve jewels; also
the scepter (*yad*), attached by a silver chain; and,
on the wooden staves of the holy scroll itself,
a golden crown (the *keter Torah*), or a smaller crown
on each of the staves, and these would be *rimónin* ("pomegranates")
of silver or gold, and ornamented with bells or lions.
A beauty! Inside your arms,
against your chest, the Word is a radiant,
touchable presence! No wonder the heart
beats quickly at that! No wonder I've seen a man in this
most sober procession nattily kick his heels
in the air and twirl! Just the two of them.
Cheek to cheek. Slow dancing.
Swaying to the music.

NaCl

A History

The trip was arduous, but it had happened
this way since the time when the gods walked Earth
and the animals spoke our language. First,
the men who were chosen to be that year's "deliverers"
underwent the-fast-of-two-days and a ritual
letting of blood. That done, they gathered their provisions
and their baskets of gold, and they left on a journey
of seven-suns-and-seven-moons . . . across a completely
waterless desert, and up to the ice-ruptured tips
of the northern ridges . . . to the "plain of exchange," where
they set out their nuggets of gold and then
retreated for the night. And in the morning
they returned, to find—tallied, as always, scrupulously—
an equal number of nuggets of salt.

Now

One day he left the headband in the truck
and all that afternoon his face seemed to be nothing
but a means for running sweat down to his eyes.
Even here, he thought, in the middle of landlocked dryfuck Kansas:
a touch of the ocean; a reminder of our home
before the lungfish. But that was his one "poetic" thought
for the week—the rest was 103° and excavating gingerly
in rubble where the bomb exploded. This
was his job, "disaster reclamation." That Sunday
he'd found the first body, a woman about his age,
her face in death become a cracked and chalky plain.
And in that first dramatic second he bent
to greet her like a lover, and his own face positively
rained on hers, grief-lit and saline.

Some Observations

How many potential separate tears, locked into the body of Lot's wife?

●

We set up the lick, and the deer seemed almost to form around it from out of the air.

●

Why is it the taste of our sorrow is so often the taste of sex?

●

We set up the lick, the deer came to it like salmon—as if returning to the source.

●

The value of a single body's puffball's-worth of elements?—barely worth calculating.

●

Barely worth calculating: yes, but tell the soul to do without this pinch that grounds its wild flight!

●

We set up the lick, and it disappeared in the deer the way that Lot's wife disappeared inside the mouth of Time.

———

This is what Dan really said one day: "They
were grazing. The moonlight held them in its pale,
limpid bond. It was so feeble
compared to the unveiled lick! We watched them
one by one lift up their heads and float off,
drawn to it like iron filings come to give some meteorite
their earthly salutations."

Intimate Past

Sally's story: people came to her for "trauma resolution."
Men, women, some who didn't know if they were men *or* women.
Her job required digging into a stranger's deepest intimate past.
At the bottom, there was always a locked box: her task was to empty it.
And they were almost physical, the thoughts she excavated.
Bloody underthings, a broken toy, a stained glove.
Here, she'd say, and hold up some monstrous thing.
This took a calm and unemotional demeanor, nearly an aridness.
You're becoming a stone, her mirror said.
And so she'd lose herself sometimes in casual sex, as a counterbalance.
"Lose" herself? — or "rediscover"?
Some of the men were sons-of-bitches; others, sweet and grateful.
That didn't matter; her transformation mattered.
She'd wake up in their arms self-baptized: new and damp and salacious.

A History

The deliverers back, the people would each receive a token
wafer of it on their tongues. And then, the annual
celebration. First, intoxicating drink;
and then the fertility dance with children
bearing cowrie shells and eggs; and then
intoxicating drink; and then intoxicating drink
with sexual intercourse; and then the ritual offering
of intoxicating drink to the dead. Then: sleep.
The full moon rose up like a Bindi dot
on the forehead of night. Then: waking. The sun,
an amber pour. Then — formally, and even
consecratingly — they'd piss in urns and drink
their piss: recycling the taste the deliverers had brought,
this necessary taste that called to their saliva.

Now

Cindy? Yes. No: not quite. He has never before
uncovered the corpse of someone that he knows; or is it
"knew"? No—Sally, *that* was her name. He knew her
for a quick but tender ask-no-questions night, one night
at a bar and then a motel in Salina, Kansas; now
this body that was under him in open generosity
is under him in this ashy debris, and *is* debris,
that he lifts to his lips and seasons
with the moisture of a last—a close to
avuncular—kiss. Then he motions a nearby crew boss over,
stoically points out his find, and returns
to the labor of digging through these hard ruins
in this hard heat: it's a job that *someone*
has to do; it's how he earns his salary.

Vessels

(Alexander von Humboldt)

In Caracas, Venezuela, in 1800, one can listen
to "the latest modern music"—Mozart, Hayden—
over sweetened ice, and Humboldt does, but once the rainy season
ends, he's off for the obdurate forests of the Orinoco,
and all of their grim amazements: streaming lengths
of anaconda, surly crocodiles, and vampire bats that hover
like nightmare hummingbirds over his hammock . . . yes,
but the greatest jawgape amazement is surely a human,
Señor del Pozo of Calabozo (a dusty
cattle-trading station), who, with no guide
but the treatise on electricity in Benjamin Franklin's *Memoirs*,
"built an electrical apparatus almost as good as the most
advanced design in the laboratories of Europe." Marvels
so often select unlikely vessels. Any alive enough

soirée should offer the example of a troll-like shnook on the arm
of a luscious hotchahotcha beauty, or the former diner waitress
with her petro-sheik amour . . . and then the tsking disbelief
of the envious rest of us. But shouldn't we *know?*
When God / His Son / His Virgin Wife decide
on a Message of Ultimate Importance for All of Mankind,
do They relay this through a group of visited
presidents, sultans, queens, and similar potentates?
Do comets spell it out, over Rio, Tokyo, mid-Manhattan?
You know. One day in a one-burro scatter of ant-swarmed shacks
in Mexico, or clutch of huts in the Urals, a mute, retarded girl
looks up from the torpor of street dogs to the sky
—and speaks. She's eloquent now with the Word, and the Way,
and the air in her wake is electric.

The S.D.G.I.E.

My friend was describing the argument. He said
she said "one single stinking sentence" that
changed everything. There was no going back.
He wouldn't repeat it for me, and yet
it's taken on the function, and the monolithic aura,
of a standard unit of measurement. The "gallon." The "light-year."
The "small domestic gesture of immense effect."

———————

On a certain predetermined night in 1843,
the country's Millerite Adventists stood in nightshirts
on their rooftops. They didn't wait on their lawns
or their second-story balconies: this was the night of the Second Coming
and the angels of this rapture were about to descend in a blizzard of wings.
As if, having journeyed from Heaven to Earth,
they might think five feet made a difference.

Stonehenge

Each morning he'd anoint the room's four corners
with an arc of piss, and then—until
he was forcibly halted—beat his forehead open
on the eastern wall, the "sunrise wall,"
incanting a doggerel prayer about God
the Flower, God of the Hot Plucked Heart; and
she, if loose in the halls, would join him,
squatting in the center of the room and masturbating
with a stolen bar of soap. This isn't *why*
they were sent to the madhouse: this is what
they needed to do *once in* the madhouse: this
is the only meaningful ritual they could fashion
there, created from the few, make-do
materials available. It isn't wondrous strange
more than the mega-boozhwah formulaic splendor
of my sister's wedding ten, eleven years ago:
her opulent bouquet of plastic flowers
(for the wilting pour of wattage at the photo session),
nigglingly arranged to match the *real* bouquet
she carried down the aisle, bloom per bloom;
the five-foot Taj Mahal of sculpted pastel sherbet;
endless "Fiddler on the Roof"; I'm sorry
now I cranked my academic sneer hauteur in place
all night. I'm sorry I didn't lose myself
like a drunken bee in a room-sized rose,
in waltzing Auntie Sally to the lush swell
of the band. We need this thing. There's not one
mineral in Stonehenge that our blood can't also raise.
One dusk, one vividly contusion-color
dusk, with my fists in my pockets and
a puzzle of fish-rib clouds in the sky, I
stopped at the low-level glow of a basement window
(Hot Good Noodle Shop) and furtively looked in:
a full-grown pig was splayed on the table,

stunned but fitfully twitching, it looked as if
it had grasshoppers under its skin. A man and a woman
slit that body jaw-to-ass with an ornate knife,
and then they both scooped out a tumble
of many dozens of wasps, preserved
by the oils of living pig to a beautiful black and amber
gem-like sheen. I saw it. Did I
see it? From inside this, over their wrists
in the tripes, they carefully removed
the wooden doll of a man and the wooden doll of a woman
maybe two inches tall, a tiny lacquered sun
and matching brass coin of a moon, and then
a child's-third-grade-version of a house
made out of pallid wax: a square of walls,
a pyramid roof, and a real smoking chimney.

A Yield

2500 years ago the poet Praxílla was called "silly" because along with the raging majesty of the sun, the stars, and the moon, she stoops to mention—as a correspondence—"cucumbers that are ripe, and pears, and apples."

This is how it usually happens: somebody dies,
or let's say almost dies, no let's say
hundreds of people die, a plane crash, swatted
out of the sky. Whatever the gods are,
they're no Jains. We're born with this
prophetic understanding coded into our neurons:
death is the payoff, death is the great motif
of this theme park of ours, and the rides are
pain and loss. And so we seek out
countervailing diversion, built to a similar scale.
Can even the great devotion house of Angkor Wat
contain such need?—"the largest
place of worship in the world," its stones
a ton apiece, its tower 215 feet
—as if it might serve for the walking-cane
of Vishnu when he visits. Will *this* suffice
to hold the omnivoracious, megalomaniac angst-&-dream
of being alive for our brief while? Will anything?
Hundreds of thousands of falcons (sacred, all)
embalmed in their pottery jars (and some
with painted plaster masks) in the beast necropolis
of ancient Saqqara. The kingdom of Prester John,
where flowed a river of gold—and a lesser river of water
ceased to flow on every Sabbath. Is there any
theophany bountifulness to suffice? The man
in the churchly shack with seven swamp-grass adders
draped in swags on his naked body. The priestess
posed like a prow at the ziggurat's top, the heart of a bull
still pulsing—with the regular beat

of a sleeping infant's breathing—
in her upheld hand. The asterisks of sun
along the bishop's mitre. Is *this* enough?
For seven decades, 35,000 workmen labored,
continuously, at once, on Versailles—the palace
at times accommodated 10,000 guests. Does any vessel
adequately stopper-up our interior roil?
Flaubert, in Egypt, exquisitely fulfilling his self-set mission
of serial sexual frolics; Kuchuk Hanem
dances the dance of "The Bee" for him, and he oohs:
"the magnificent absolutely sculptural design of her knees."
Is *this* enough? Is any Taj Mahal or Alhambra
ever enough? He enters her: "like rolls of velvet," he calls it
"as she made me come." And then it's the end of the day:
"She falls asleep with her hand in mine.
She snores." The bishop removes his mitre,
it looks like a fairyland dollhouse now.
The priestess sits at her bowl of oiled rice and leeks
like anyone, and massages her feet.
At the end of a day of volcanoes
and aurora borealis, the physical universe
attends to the completeness of every molecular bond
in every knuckle of gravel on a garden path.
This path. . . . A man has walked
across the surface of the moon, and has returned,
to ticker-tape parades and magnums of champagne,
with a bag of its sharp-faced mineral treasures.
Now it's twenty years later. He stands in a garden,
any man in a backyard garden, holding a rock,
considering it, then
placing it just-so. The sun descends,
and for a moment is an egg glaze over everything.
Inside the house, at the basement utility sink,
he scrubs each cucumber of his yield individually.
(Upstairs—the sounds of his wife in the kitchen,
footsteps, shut drawers, so familiarly organized
to his ear by now that they register as a music.
Outside—the regular neighborhood thrum.)
Each one is striped green like a race car,
holding its clear and clement juice in its body.
Ordinary beauty. You could cry.

Far

1.

A docu-film from 1912: a shaman
of the western steppes is "traveling
in the Land of Ghosts." What that means is
he's twitching on the ground like a voltage wire
discharging wildly, and the effort of it
overflows his jaws in sour foam.
It isn't pretty, but it's credible at least
—more so, for me, than this medieval altar painting
where the newly dead are welcomed into Heaven
through what seems to be a middle-class reception line
of angels in their freshly laundered robes: it's all
less alien, less distant,
than our camping trips just sixty minutes south of here,
when wings of darkness settle in the dark boughs.
After all, what *are* the standard rules of measurement
for "far"? In that cartoon by Charles Addams,
his severe, sepulchral characters are gathered on a roof:
the uncle's stretched out on his stomach
in attempt to get a "moontan," and a toadstool's started growing
from his back. I think this tells us
that the map of us, of what's not yet explored in us,
will never be unfolded to completion. As for "close at hand". . .
that shaman is a dynamo of thrashing
right in front of us, so *very* here, so adamantly eloquent
of "hereness," loud, immediate. Although
look in his eyes: he's somewhere else.

2.

Then E. returned, her face smashed in and burnt
in the shape of a clothes iron. Close up,
hugging her, we could smell it
drifting off her skin in sick, crisp curls.

"No, it wasn't no iron." Seven weeks
that she'd been missing, without a word—now this.
"The Martians did it." She said.
No one believed her of course, not the cops,
her friends, or Roy, but that was her story,
that was her cover story, self-repeated
into the durability of myth. "They sucked me
sky-high to their ship like pop up a straw." Wherever
she'd wandered, and whoever they were, the psychic mileage
may as well be logged in interplanetary units.
And D. returned—this was a year, to the day,
from the strict gray afternoon of his mother's funeral—
and he wasn't the same, though none of us
could articulate *how*, exactly. We didn't know
where he'd been: one rumor was a West Coast cult,
hooded robes and weird devotional rites,
but nobody *knew*. His mind . . . the D.-self
still remained, but was reordered,
like the shook dice of a word game. Not that
leaving is always a matter of fracture; Swedenborg
suggests that, after dying, the Eternity
we enter is a bridged continuation of our lives,
the lawns, the sacheted drawers of underthings.
There's a glory, an ethereal glory, about it; and yet
the structures haven't changed. "Well, it's,"
a beautiful woman said to me once, "like stepping
out of a hot bath into Louisiana in August."

3.

There are fifteenth-century printed books
where we can see pieces of type are left
embedded in the paper. One more proof of how
our origins are a telltale presence inside us;
on *some* level, ineradicably. My Grandma Rosie's
accent said that it came from the deep
of a dented tub of chicken blood, and was also
there at the other tub as the clothes were stirred
with a crooked oar-like stick to a semblance of cleanliness
—the "old country." Old, low, garlic-scented

moans; the "evil eye"; old handkerchief dancing.
And yet that world was ever-present in Chicago
—a kind of archeological layer—under
even her thickest crust of lilac-scented
dime-store *Nuit d'Amor* bath powder and under
the atomized drizzle of its accompanying cologne.
By then she'd had too many intimate talks
with a God who Himself smelled thickly
of herring scales smeared beneath
His fingernails . . . that sensibility
never lost its claim upon her citizenship.
I see, now, how her difficult displacement
to America was met, each day, with a series
of small heroics; back then, however, when she
was still alive, she was simply a living embarrassment.
You know how in a comic book a flying superduperguy
will zoom across the sky and land with a trail
behind him of sketchy, half-transparently rendered
outlines of himself as signifier of his path? That's
how I picture her: in front of me
with an arch of numerous overlapping "hers"
extending back unbroken to dirtstreet Europe.
I think it would only have been as her casket
entered the ground, and my father stood there
with the ashy aftertaste of the mourner's prayer
on his tongue, and then the soil was topped off
and tamped even, that she would have risen,
along that great curve, just before
it vanished, at last returned to her source.

4.

It seems insufficient to offer it
as any kind of profundity—*When something ends,
something else begins*—but it's the premise
supporting an afterlife that's been with us
since the first of our cadavers were daubed
in ocher tinting (red=blood?=birth?) and bent
against the grain of rigor mortis
into the trifold curl we've come to designate

the fetal position; the flowers
placed with purpose on top of these burials from before
we were technically "human" may be equally a gesture
of farewell *and* the earliest record that we have
of the sentiment *bon voyage*. And also in minor
and mundane ways: when X and I
were dead to each other as lovers, we were very much
alive in newer love vignettes,
both geographic and psychological
states away from where and who we were
that sultry August in Louisiana—'Weeziana,
as she'd say. But the quality of that kind
of lickerish mingling can't be measured
by the calendar; and those were glorious days.
There aren't many times I've seen the light itself
take on a fully fleshly weight; in stained-glass
saints, of course; perhaps throughout the beam,
the living banister, that ran the length
of the dark in an old-time movie house; and certainly
in the humidity of the Gulf Coast, over X's body
languorously resting after sex. And why "we"
didn't survive? . . . well, each of us was ligatured
invisibly but durably to someone else.
For me, a woman so much farther north,
she wrote that she already woke, sometimes, this early,
to a petitpoint of snow upon the grass. And X? . . .
was tethered to a man whose grave she'd stood at
as they shoveled it closed only ten months before.
A long leash of belonging.
I'd helped her shiver in pleasure;
I'd rolled her in the dew.
And every time I shook her . . .
he shook her too.

5.

Another film of the shamans of the tribes
of the western steppes: they're in a stately,
slow procession—it's the Walk of Conversation
With the Dead—and every now and then, one

disappears (a function of the sheets
of fog among the trees), then reappears
a few feet farther. Nothing now
will make me think that they can choose to talk
with Grandma Rosie, or that *any* of the old,
depleted tales of gods and remnant spirits
still has voice enough to call us ably
to the holy places, the foot of the mountain,
the cave of sighs, the water where the sun sets.
No, it's just that I remember her
explaining to a three-year me the logic
of the stitching that, from pleasure or necessity,
she worked at every day. "You see?"
She pointed where the thread dropped out.
"It's visiting the other side."

Gone

Stationed

It's the other ones, who soon enough return
to being happy after the funeral, that are nearest
to their own deaths — in their gaiety
and everyday distraction, they're so open

and unguarded . . . *anything* could enter them;
could claim them. It's the ones who weep
incessantly that are saved for now, the ones
who have taken a little of it

into their systems: this is how
inoculation works. And sorrow is difficult,
a job: it requires time to complete.
And the tears? — the salt

of the folk saying,
that gets sprinkled over the tail feathers
and keeps a bird from flying;
keeps it stationed in this world.

Remains Song

The penis is gone, the penis of even *Tyrannosaurus rex*
is gone, the hardest of them all is only oleo
to time, and disappears, with the tongue,
and the brain, and its beehive of thought, and the portentous
vaginal lips, and their promise: vanished,
enzymatically, molecularly: gone. Although

the bone that anchored the "penis retractor muscle"
is a small rib in the towering, vaulted, domed
cathedral of dinosaur infrastructure that
remains—and, by its telltale osseous presence, we
can clarify our muddy paleobiological guesses at
Cretaceous sex. The jazzman's breath

is gone, but the saddle of callus is still intact
on the cadaver's lip: a fossil of pain,
of fucked-up pimped-down pain, and of the rapture
when we're blown like smoke rings out of ourselves
at 4 A.M. in cellarlight and sweat until there's no
"ourselves," there's only a haze on the stage. The rapist

is gone, but his signature DNA remains in the bloody wads
beneath her fingernails. The physicist is gone,
but light remains, its relativity and speed remain,
confounding us anew like the thwack of a barrel stave
against our heads each morning. The marriage
is gone, but the baby is seven pounds, three ounces

and screaming its shitty little petal-pretty skull off
in the bedroom. When the atmosphere is left below,
the air still *sishes* out of the 747's overhead nozzles. Then
something goes wrong. The plane is an untranslatable scatter
of metal debris and burnt flesh; but
the black box is an eloquence. The flint tool

is a proof of the hand that wielded it: the hand is only
so many atoms of carbon now, some water, and
a coppery ancestral taste when we're licking each other's bodies.
And the moment of conception, of the universe's
becoming the universe, twenty billion of units we call "years"
ago, is lost, although the scream of this,

the fire of this, the pattern, and the radial awayness, these
are life as we move through it daily.
As we move through it daily we're always, somewhere,
gone. House dust is 70%
shed human skin, and what we breathe in is a whiff
of the extinguished. Here in Dinosaur Hall

our detective hero is woefully bamboozled: someone's
stolen a famous thigh bone the size of a Greyhound bus,
and though this room is nothing but structured
evidential testimony to life-forms from millennia
back—and posed with the seeming immediacy of centerfolds—
he can't find one hard clue to a felon who's history

by only sixty minutes. Later that night, alone
at home, he lists the facts repeatedly. Of course
alone. You're happy, you're together, then something
goes wrong. He knows that now. He studies her empty
half of the closet. Eerily: aren't these hangers something like the wire
a museum dioramacist fashions a torso around? . . . He

studies her porcelain coffee cup, still here in the sink . . .
her lip-print on its rim. . . . To him, her cyst was
extradition to another world. "Another world"—and
we're *its* archeology, its ongoing Ur or Assyria.
"She's with God now," the priest said—frowning, as if
God were a boy-toy neighbor she'd decided to run off with.

(Untitled)

I remember, from my childhood, seeing the miners
pull a bucket up to the light
from their lowermost levels, working
rope against its wishes,
working to spite the law of gravity,
hand over hand. And when the bucket arrived? . . .
they emptied it, then lowered it,
then readied again for the long pull. And
my mother's irrefusable breathing,
there at the last of the cancer.

Packing for a Difficult Trip,

I take my sci-fi paperback adventure
—I can lose myself agreeably
inside its brawling cosmos; and,
to balance that, a pedantically serious treatise
on the measurement of time in preliterate cultures;
and a book of verse . . . trying to anticipate
varieties of reading need
—"intended for use on occasions
yet to arise," so says the treatise,
of early shaped stone stored in caves.
If she's in pain, I'll divert her with stories.
If she dies, I'll be strong for my sister's sake.
Preparing preparing preparing. Now getting
onto the flight to Chicago.

The Sonnet for Planet 10

My mother is dying. Nothing
halts the cancer's steady spread;
despite some talky knee-jerk optimists
in the family, she won't leave from the nursing home
for *her* home, ever. *I'm* there, though,
in a sad half-zomboid try to sort its recent scraps.
A pink note double-magneted to the fridge, *call Ruthie Lakin;*
an appointment at the oncology center
(never now to be kept); *Remember Livia's b'day;*
last week's unthumbed *TV Guide*, and last month's
crossword puzzle magazine, with its untenanted squares
—a life's unfinished business,
far more eloquent for me than even
those incomplete statues of Michelangelo's,
always breaking and never breaking
out of their origin stone. Do you remember
the excitement over word that a new,
tenth planet was thought to exist? There wasn't one,
of course, and yet by now the very possibility
of its being with us—the promise of it, the weird allure—
orbits up there anyway, and is one of the century's
famous unkept deadlines. *That's*
where I'm going to dump the rummage sale announcement,
and the reminder card from the dentist,
and the leftover Swiss in its strip of tinfoil wrap:
on Planet 10, right next to the meadow of graven monuments
that feature the text of everything
she and I have never said to each other. This poem
was going to be a sonnet—unfinished, diminished,
burial, funereal, etc.
But I'm weary, and I'm leaving it undone.

The Gunshot in the Parking Lot:

is a pop in that vast public space, a dot
that doesn't make it to the evening news.
And the sound of my mother raging at the orderly
forcibly peeling her off her wet sheets, "No,
I'm stuck, it hurts me, no"—the cancer
was planting its bulbs in her body, but
her mind was clear, was pitilessly clear,
and she knew that a tangle of needled tubes
had snared her ankle, knew this hidden snag the orderly
was blind to—"You must listen to me!"
in that ever-thinning whisper of hers, as the orderly
continued yanking and down the hall the barking of a human
kennel started up, "You must listen
to me!" her voice lost in the general din and disdain.

The Gold Star

Elaine's job on the geriatric ward included encouraging
the constipated to loose their stingy, gnarled marbles
into the bowl—by hand: there wasn't anything more tenderly
conducive than an orderly's gloved fingers.
There's nothing redeeming in this. Simply: she
needed the pay, they needed her excavating
(literally: *from out / of their cavities*) help.
The rest?—"an alien stink that followed me home,
under my toenails, in my hair." But surely we'd do it
willingly for someone that we loved . . . yes? Even
gratefully—for someone that we loved. And then
we'd clean the pad, we'd rinse it free of its gobbets
the size and color of cornelian cherries . . .
gladly, yes? Gladly and changed. Better;
tested. Even when my mother was dying,
shrinking, growing hard rosettes
as if her lungs were tanks in an experiment . . .
didn't I tend to her? and wasn't it the way
it always used to be?—that with precision instinct
she'd arranged this just so she could prove
to relatives and neighbors that her son
was so caring, her son was the best. I'd wring
the compress, set it on her forehead again.
What a good boy I was!

The Sequel to "The Sonnet for Planet 10"

An assistant . . . helped the police solve a major theft by identifying the
source of rocks that had been used to fill crates. . . . He helped solve a sim-
ilar case by identifying where a load of sand came from.
                                                —Douglas J. Preston

This three-inch glazed ceramic shoe
with the coyly inquisitive glazed ceramic cat astride it
was manufactured in Dresden. The Bible
in Haifa, and the chalkware tabletop Buddha
who looks a little like the latter-day porker Elvis
in Taiwan. The chalk in the pressing
transmutational weight of the sea. The clay
in the buried sea below the topographical contrivance
we call Germany. The sea in the first configuration
of elements spun in the stars. When meteorites
hit air they typically whistle or hum,
and one observer in Rose City, Michigan, in 1921,
is reported saying, "I distinctly heard
fine singing." Swirls in the meteorite
that fell near the Rio del Valle de Allende in 1969
are mineral proof it originated
in astral dust clouds older than the solar system.
But this is getting far from a man
in a small house on North Washtenaw today,
who's organizing what the lawyer calls
his mother's "effects."[*] It ought to be simple,
a box for *save*, a box for *sell*, but everything
he touches is suddenly eloquent of a spacetime nexus
larger than itself. Or maybe he just doesn't *want*
to think of her gone. I know, because
he's me; because the dull and pitted cleaver
in the chopping bowl is heightened by death

with the pent-in charge we normally think
would sizzle the tip of a finger
touched to an unearthed relic from Sumer.
And what of the "hatful of English pennies,
several rivets, a bunch of keys, a half-crown,
and a bobby's whistle?"—these were retrieved
from the stomach of Barnum's vastly famous Jumbo
at the elephant's dissection. Yes, but that's
their easiest provenance, and it gets more complicated,
of course, the way what we see in the sky at night
is light so old its source is often dead.
That's too much "much" for me. I'm
going to sleep for an hour or so
in my mother's bed. I'm going to be like glass
that dreams it's sand again, and sand that dreams
it's once again a living vein in the planet.

---

* Which then would make her their "cause," I suppose: a kind of etiolology.

On the Beach with the Vikings

He was known for his "slow burn" shtick
—a local comedian, a wonder
wowing the small-club circuit
years ago, and now (a buried one-inch notice
on page 11 tells us)

dead. And just last night in the attic
I was thinking about his funny, consumptive
anger: it was all that boxed-up paper
there, destroying itself
from inside, from its own component acids

over time, over long, insistent time
. . . slow burn. Finally, the smoking did that
to my mother, and her lungs became
two brambles converting themselves to ash.
If this is a riddle, the answer is

at my window. It's September. This tree
is nearing the end of its journey, blazing
red by yellow, day by day: the stately corpse
of the king, as well as the funeral ship on fire
—in one.

Apology

I don't know what connects the different poetries
of Jane Kenyon and Larry Levis, unless
it's love of life so rich it can afford
to love the weeping at its center. And,

of course, that both of them are dead now,
early. How we *want* to read their work
for strength that's independent
of the happenstance

of elegiac context . . . which is what
I try to have my students see
in Plath and Keats, although I lie:
we *can't* read purely, to the point

where we will separate the great, exclamatory
words of Shelley from the sea-reek
of his body in the rocks upon the shore. Nor
will we ever read Anne Sexton anymore

without the tailpipe. I write this in apology
to Jane and Larry, poets who
deserve a reading better than we bring.
And William Matthews too.

The Lives of the Artists

"She accomplished the incredible feat of painting
the most sentimentally fraught of subjects
—mother and child—without one thimble of sentimentality."
That, of Mary Cassatt. If long is true, her looking
never lied, it stayed so faithfully with its subject.
Or: it's 1879. His wife Camille is on her deathbed.
And "I found myself, without being able to help it,
in a study of my beloved wife's face," reports
Monet in self-tormented confession,
"systematically noting the colors." Looking. Getting out
the whetted edge of his looking and paring the skin
of light itself, to see light's underside. This
must be something akin to what makes Lot's wife
turn. The risk. The call of accuracy. To witness.

Maypurés

One nova recorded by Tycho Brahe continued, by virtue of his eminence, "to be shown on celestial globes long after it had disappeared from the sky."

—Adrian Johns

And so a lacquered, giltwork wooden globe
an ostler could have toyed with—about
the circumference of a soccer ball—contained
the same misleadingly fixative powers as the whole
of outer space: that star was long dead
by the time of its observation. Also,
two years after Reynolds's funeral, Lyla's
mynah continued to squawkle his name and a certain
intimacy of theirs—a burr in her brain
whenever she heard it, a burr on fire
in the middle of her thinking. In a way,
a poem that still holds on to "ostler" as a currency
is much like those celestial globes.
"Bistre." "Halberd." "Biffin." "Clyster." —Words
that require an asterisked footnote under the actual
body of the text. That's what a ghost is,
yes?—it tugs at our attention, but
it's no longer part of the ongoing body. One night
I attempted consoling Lyla, who'd phoned
in a panic: she thought she'd seen him again,
composed of the unearthly blue
that wavers in a match flame,
"and so help me God I started to talk about my day
as if he really stood there." And what *does* one say
to a friend whose sorrow is somebody gone
below the level of breath, beyond

the bonds inside the atom? Facts
won't help, although I did
suggest her own grief had the kinship of a hundred thousand
counterparts. Humboldt tells a story
about the "famous parrot of Maypurés; the last speaker
of the language of the Atures tribe had vanished, therefore
no one could understand the poor bird"—a footnote
in his travel journals. "Asterisk":
a little star. In this case, one whose heart burns up
in reference to nothing.

Futures

The sky is nearly plaided with the speedy traffic
of boomerang-shaped, one-family (or sportier) airmobiles
on the cover of the sci-fi book he's reading, he being
fourteen. He can't abide the present moment, it's so
. . . crummy, really crummy. He can't start
to see his own next twenty years, whatever
compromise and common, almost begrudgingly kept, fidelities
it's sure to hold. And so he's all of a thousand years
ahead of the rest of his sleeping household,
dreamily leaping over the pinnacled surface of other planets
in silvery gravi-boots: a woman to rescue,
a Star Alliance robo-ship to save. A thousand years

———————————

ago (A.D. 922) the envoy Ibn Fallan witnessed
"the girl who devoted herself to death" be
stabbed, and then pyred alongside a Viking chief
while, otherwheres, one Luitprand of Cremona (A.D. 950 or so)
was delivered "on the shoulders of two eunuchs"
into the presence of the Emperor of Constantinople, whose throne,
"anon, did float in the air above me." Wonders. Atrocities
and wonders. And though they couldn't foretell the simple
rrrip of a Velcro strip, or the tick of an engine cooling down
like the pawl on a slowing carnival wheel, still
these ancient chroniclers would recognize our own
ongoing fears, small courage, and sleeplessness. Speaking

———————————

of which: while I've been diverting us, someone's awakened.
His mother. She rarely sleeps for more than an hour
now, from the lump's extending its spidery legs.
The doctor says: six months. And so at night she carefully
plans the listed details of her own funeral. The music,
the floral decor (by *individual blossom*), the opening poem.
Her own sure, heart-of-hearts choice for the latter is
Dylan Thomas's "And Death Shall Have No Dominion"
—such a painful, lavish, spilled-out bag of language!—but
her Women's Support Group thinks a "woman poet" more
appropriate, and wields subtle pressures men
would never be allowed. After all, the battle is never over;

there's so much left to be done.

Some Deaths That Have Recently Come to My Attention

Premature and only nineteen ounces, Sonny
shouldn't even have lived those six
precarious and lovingly tended-to months
he somehow did. The service went
like this: everyone was given a lily
—a hundred of us—and then was ushered
into a sumptuous chamber, at the front of which
an open, empty casket had been placed.
And then the father entered, walking down
the center aisle with Sonny's body
held in his extended arms. He didn't look
like a mourner, exactly—more as if
we witnessed him carrying some
incomprehensible and wondrous thing
he'd just found in the woods,
and brought inside, for us to explain it,
here in our civilized room.

———————————

My mother's death has also recently come
to my attention. Not that I wasn't there
six years ago, in the nursing home,
when her life shrank to the size of an eye
and closed. And I was there at the slow,
slow closing of that other eye:
her grave. And yet each *new* death
brings *her* death back fresh,
with a slap, as if I'd forgotten it
—as if, for the important deaths,
a tiny—a lowercase—alzheimer's
beats it out of our memory
every minute, so that
every minute it's new again.

And the unknown deaths . . .
the newspaper stats,
the distant sirens splitting the night. . . .
Not name acts.
Only the house bands of death.

If there's any common denominator,
it might be in the story
of Copernicus's dying:
that he first received a copy
of his printed book
while on his deathbed, seeing it,
as George Eliot says, "as a dim object
through the deepening dusk."
It's finally everybody's story
—a hand reaches out
and, just as it does, the whole
universe slips away.

How I Want to Go

1.

One way would be
almost without transition: water,
rising out of water,
as water, isn't aware of the moment
(well, there *isn't* "a" moment) it turns
to air.
      But a letter from Rick, which came today
from brambled Scottish highland, says
that the hawk can sense exactly where
the rabbit's heart is beating—is an aerothermal
system of pinpoint location—
"then it stamps its talon into the heart,
as easily as an olive is speared."
So that would be another way:
the poison dart of my personal angel
of death come down to lift me.

2.

The newspaper coverage said that they were "making love"
in the road, when they were killed by a spill of hundreds
of "chalkware figurines" off the sloppily loaded flatbed
that they'd impulsively left idling on the shoulder . . . but I'm here
to tell you frankly they were pure and simple
fucking—in the cleansing heat
of that animal need—and found butt-naked
under a mound of gaudy elephant-headed gods
the color of blueberry icing . . . and an equal number
of vapidly beaming Infants of Prague with spray-paint halos
set in their heads like fancy pleated dinner napkins,
and tutu-pink plump cheeks. —A new world standard
for "ignominious."

But this serves
to remind me of its countervailing image,
from a sheaf of Victorian photographs: a stillborn boy,
the size of a catalpa leaf, and set
in the casket under such a weight of gilt embroidery,
they must have feared this elfin thing
would otherwise have floated away.
It didn't live long enough for the midwife
even to wipe the womb-cheese from its eyes.
Its total experience was the cutting of the cord.

3.

EMO! [*eéy-mo*]: what, one year, the "cool guys"
(jerks) in junior high kept yelling in the hallways
and covertly inking over the walls: acronymically,
Eat Me Out. It made no sense to me. First,
wasn't this command what the woman would say, not the man?
Was this supposed to be some witticism put forth
ventriloquially? And second, cunnilingus was desirable,
a pleasure—yes? Then why did this utterance
enter the world as if it were an insult? That year,
everything was confusing.
                    For example, my Aunt Regina
was dying, making her departure
an ordeal of miscued neural paths
and failed speech, as measured in extra millimeters
per day of unstoppable, hardening cells. The cancer,
one of the doctors shrugged and said, was eating out her brain.

4.

This started with the ocean:
water rising out of water. But that's not
the only image of ascending to be found
along the beach or out on the blue expanse itself.
Some fish will fight their being hooked up
with a violent, body-snapping will: the cunning
and determination make of them something

beyond themselves, like a person suddenly
filled with a god. I've seen a marlin
(just as inland, once, a sturgeon) thrash
a two-man boat to its destruction. The fish know:
this is their silt, their own worm-threaded dearestness,
and *nothing* is going to force them out. I've
been here watching a sunset tonight
—how each wave is a heartbeat of a cup
that holds this golden glow—and I've decided I want to go
complaining and resistant and requiring
of effort to get: the way the meat
leaves the leg of a crab.

Some Cloths

1.

The color wrung out of a wrung-out cloth, a flock of city pigeons on the roof is no one's notion of exalting. Lumped like wads of used-up hankie tissue, littered on prodigiously beshitted tiles . . . who could work up interest in their lax—their close to coma'd—doze in the vitiating late-afternoon Wichita sun?

But then a cue—invisible to me, and silent—clicks them into shared awareness . . . and, as one, they lift in the single undulant length of some Baghdadian flying carpet: keeping that roughly oblong shape, they sleek their aerial way throughout the maze that city skyline spires, antennae, and towers are to a flight of birds. They're one communal motion now, all zip and grace and speedy slink.

Invisible to me, and silent. . . . Not a sign: there wasn't any slam I heard, there wasn't any sudden, overlooming dangershadow, nor could I detect their alpha-pigeon shrugging subtle coded orders backward down his shabby ranks. Whatever it was, it passed for spontaneity. However it worked, its nanoincremental links engaged themselves somewhere below my threshold of perception . . . the same unknowable level where magic cooks, before the allakazzam of its being served well-done on stage; the place where quantum physics zizzles with its here-then-not-here, if-and-almost, sub- and anti-particles.

Amitov Ghosh: "For about five hundred years Aidhab functioned as one of the most important halts on the route between the Indian Ocean and the Mediterranean. Then, suddenly, in the middle of the fifteenth century its life came to an end: it simply ceased to be, as though it had been erased from the map. The precise cause of its demise is uncertain." *That's* the level I'm talking about!—where cities-sundering vectors of climate / high priests / economic curves / political alliances . . . exercise themselves, like fault lines, miles under our ability to notice . . . except, of course, for the effects of those accumulated movements, finally immanent in the terms of our daily world. A city: vanished. A *city*: lost to sight as easily as a hen's egg up a magician's sleeve.

And in fact the magician reminds us that my reverie on Aidhab is misleading in scale. Every second, every inch, it happens; every time the atoms of a solid, any solid, decide—if "decide" is the word—to remain inside the field of the molecules of that solid, it happens. Under our notice: it happens. Here, in the world of our notice: we have "stone" / have "cloth" / have "flesh." A rush of pigeons: "rush" as a singular noun.

Below the table, inside the dark, the dozen unremarkable, preparatory steps get made. What *we* see is the bird in its astonishing arc from below the conjuror's hat, flapping in the air like a jellabeya snagged on a summer day's wind.

2.

One dandy understanding the politicians are pleased to have (and put to use) is that they *don't* have to lie: if only two half-truths are placed in a smartly artful proximity, *we'll* fill in the blank between them. What the brain has been evolved to do: make wholeness. It's how movies work: the brain makes continuity out of two distinctly separate visual units. "Life" and "afterlife": the mind imagines a link called "the soul," and moves it (often with a rich religious drama) across a ligature of its own devising. Give us point A-1 and point A-2, and we'll elide, we couldn't *not*.

It may be thirty-seven pigeon-language signifiers that ultimately get those birds airborne; and it may be a process that, to the view of a god or a hawk or a moon rock, is a staggered and gradual thing; no doubt, the orchestration of optic nerve and hormone-trigger and muscle-contracting across the population of a rooftop flock is multi- and omni- and pan-. And yet for us it's one gray tablecloth pulled off the roof: a *snap*.

And what of the fires that were burning up my Auntie Hannah, eighty-nine? — alone in the world (except for myself and my sister) and alone in its representative space for her: a Medicare hospital bed. "It's burning me up alive," she'd tell us seven, eight times in an hour; we could see the surface of her shrivel and blotch, her tongue crack in the act of speech. But no one — and here I'm including the corps of indifferent medical specialists — could see inside remedially to the cause. Those fires licking her clean were each just the size of one cell in her body. Every nucleus in her had its own inferno, somewhere underneath the line that separates the unknown from the comprehended. Calling this by a latinate name, a textbook designation weighty in syllables, didn't *explain* it at all.

And what of the dinosaurs? Something gigantic, naturally, it would have to be: the impact of a comet, at least, a crash the size of an ocean. Although the lesson of *The War of the Worlds* is that the monstrous military might of Mars is vanquished by a sneeze. It seems ridiculous to say it, it's so obvious: an invisible comet is equally unseeable as an invisible microbe.

Macrobe: why isn't *that* a word? Those ancient Mayan cities that were emptied of their populations seemingly overnight, the way a chrysalis is left behind, or the jettisoned flesh of the Rapture . . . these are terraces, though, and altars and avenues . . . monuments and granaries and hallways of empiric power . . . those cities with names that sound so exotically floral to our ears, that hint at such exotic appetites: emptied of their people in the blink of a Mayan eye, abandoned and left behind like sloughed stone skins . . . with no clue of invasion, revolt, or rampaging disease. Whatever rock it was that toppled this Goliath of an ancient urban network, it's as deep beneath our notice as the algae in the bodies of the polyps that, by thousands, make a branch of coral we hold as if it's a single and uniform thing.

It's what I do with these two photographs—eighty-five years apart—of Auntie Hannah. She's four in the first, a wide-eyed child stiffly standing in a checked dress (with a matching bow in her hair of such enormity it looks like a lavish Amazonian jungle moth that's preening on a tiny cake-top figurine). In the second—only a month ago—she's eighty-nine, and already almost smudgily translucent in her illness; there are patches of tarnish under her eyes and, under her skin, the look of heavy webbing. What I do in my mind is fill in the blank between. I reminisce—invent, extrapolate, and reminisce—and make, between those poles, the bridging arc we call "biography." "A life."

"Knock on wood for me, kiddo." Right: "wood"; "diamond"; "brick"—as if in these we'll come upon a final, an unparsable, solidity to count on. Sure: as if that hard, impervious shape way off in the sky—that thick dark bolus—doesn't settle down somewhere on a rooftop as a scatter of birds

3.

Amitov Ghosh: "I would go up to my room alone and listen to the call of the muezzin and try to think of how it must feel to know that on that very day, as the sun travelled around the earth, millions and millions of people in every corner of the globe had turned to face the same point, and said exactly the same words of prayer, with exactly the same prostrations as oneself."

The phototropic cells in a leaf. The gawkers at the premiere, as the sex goddess exits her limo: a star, and its magi.

On the all-nude side at Showtime Lounge, the strobes and the series of lights along the apron of the stage, and of course the poses of the dancers themselves, are all arranged to finally funnel attention to the erotico-gynelogical vee— shaved, this year, and often clit-ringed: there's no end to sexual fashion. The women are prideful, playful, paid well; and the men—whether only two or a full two hundred—are a single organism, a hive of an eye, obedient, following.

After a while, of course, the novelty wears off. And when a dancer steps offstage at the end of her three-song set, and opens the door to the wardrobe room—a sudden column of light in the relative dark, which marks the entrance to a world that's still forbidden to the audience—it's interesting to see the head of every man automatically turn to the door's six seconds of teasing promise, turn as if practiced, choreographed . . . perhaps we could say evolution *is* a million years of practice . . . as if this slice out of the darkness might reveal some amazing bodily sanctum even beyond the naked force of the official show.

On the roof of the building across from Auntie Hannah's room they land, then rise and circle like a kite, then land and individuate in the sun for a while, then rise and circle. All morning I watch them . . . when I'm not watching her, in her stuttering half-sleep. This is the time, her time, of breaking back to the body's constituent elements. This is the time of their being released.

And even so, she's alive again today. Is that good? There's some pain, but we still think it's good. My sister pats her forehead dry, then we both help Auntie Hannah sit up. "You know," she says, "I'll be with Uncle Lou soon." That's a chilling thought to me, but hey: this isn't about me. Auntie Hannah's smiling, as if she's just said a wonderful, comforting thing.

It's a morning of little miracles. For instance, the atoms inside the glass she drinks from . . . which aren't *so* different from the atoms in the air, or the walls, or my prickled skin . . . they *all* came from the furnace hearts of stars . . . the atoms inside the glass remain in the glass, cohere, don't effervesce away, and the glass is a glass.

The wall is the wall: a real nail could really be driven into it. My skin is my skin. The sheet on her body remains the sheet, as stable a shape as that square of birds, which rises now, a prayer shawl in the air, a wedding canopy.

The Children

Myth Studies

The custodian erases whatever simple biology
lesson was on the blackboard: BIRTH.
It's only a several-seconds glimpse I've had
through a door on my way to the car, but enough
for me to think of him as the Saint
of First-Time Mothers. What I mean is,
after the walls split, and the screams stopped,
and Atlantis disappeared, another Atlantis
—the one we carry in our heads, of scented gardens
and ornate avenues—fills the emptiness.
I've seen it in my friends: the terrible
pelvis-wrenching pain is at an end, and then
some chemical washes the mind, and creates
the blankness of fresh possibility.

(Untitled)

We call it birth, but it's also as if
the mother becomes the shed skin
of a first existence.

                           I love the way
that when the crayfish loses its shell,
you can see the life in its new translucent body
kick like a dog in sleep.

Cord

What can I compare them to, five years later, except their child
drawn from the vaginal sleeve with the umbilicus slipped
around its throat? Its color, cyanotic; but
it lived. Retarded. Loveable—oh yes, loveable
and endlessly demanding, in the way of that kind
of love. Fulfilling; and monolithically central.
Something always needed, some immense unasked-for
sacrifice to make. And that's become their whole
existence—you can see the life-cord twisted thickly around their necks,
the everyday-to-day cord. Just as it is for all of us, though a little
more invisibly than theirs. To live with that cord is a tiny death;
to sever it, quicker and worse.

Children / Expediencies

The purpose of a pen: to write.
The purpose of a bottle: to store; to pour from
—though my mother would also make them
doll-sized dressmaker's forms, displaying frocks
of calico or gingham on bottles of ketchup;
and once I saw an emptied bottle of champagne
used in a porno flick (beyond description here),
another mother of invention being
venality. We love to find ingenious,
extra functions: show me a lemon
and I'll show you a stain remover. What's
the "purpose," for example, of a child?
To become an adult? To save a marriage?
As many reasons as children, I think.

———————

And one was loved on barley-water and cabbage,
just as one was loved on wetnurse-milk
and candied breast of swan. Another suffered
to have his back implanted with tufts of fur
from a dog, so earned his keep in a circus
—Hans the Dancing Bear Boy. At the same time,
one was born to be the god of his people:
leaning on a pillow of lotus petals, on a throne of gold,
ten years old and nodding *yes* or *no* to the room of councillors.
And the story of the woman who'd inherit her fortune
only if she "gave" her parents a grandchild.
Well, she did—with the mailman. It was a boy.
She chose his name: Invention,
and had hers legally changed: Necessity.

The kettle that was hammered into a helmet.
The note from a prisoner of war that was written
in ink he mixed from blood and coal dust.
And the shipdeck nails hammered into wedding rings
for two of the marooned on a desert isle. I relish
tales of useful expediencies. Remember in line 1
I wrote "to write"?—in 1926,
a man by the name of John Carter was born
in the village of Ware (just north of London) weighing
a dismal 3.4 pounds. This is what he says:
"They laid me on a hot-water bottle,
wrapped me in cotton
soaked in cod-liver oil, and fed me
brandy through the nib of a fountain pen."

D___ L___'s

Fathers are invariably great nuisances on the stage, and always have to give the hero or heroine a long explanation of what was done before the curtain rose, usually commencing with "It is now nineteen years, my dear child, since . . ." &tc. &tc.

—Charles Dickens

There might be a planet. Before that,
though, there would have been a gas that coalesced
into a planet . . . as, before *that*, there were dots of flux
and energy that hadn't yet declared themselves
in concert. There's always "before": there's more
each minute, more each person, yes and every one
of its smallest, irreducible subparticles—which I name
the "beforeon"—is exerting force on us
that's surely time's own version of gravity: its purpose
is to tug, and to remind us. In the house of second marriages,

it causes the man to do what he and the woman had promised
they never would: one night while she's asleep, he snoops
her bureau for telltale relics of the mysterious Mr.
Number One. And why, or even what
he hopes to find, he couldn't clearly say: a letter? photo?
sex toy?—*something*, some objectified gossip, a fossil
of bygone love. Essentially, we make of our own psyches
a bureau and pay a shrink to snoop; as for the moment
when our neural linkage first began to form,
as for the flavor of the fluids in the womb . . . we're all

amnesiacs: and our earliest self, just like the universe's
earliest being, is a "phantom limb" with the faintest
mnemonic of starbursts in an otherwise chill void. I have
a friend D___ L___ (this poem is hers) who, orphaned
as a newborn, is devoted to learning her origin

as doggedly as any cosmologist tracks light to its source, although
her search (when not pure Internet) is more a matter
of tape-recording the beer-sour stories in sailor bars,
of sifting ashy memories in nursing homes,
one backwards inch of plotline at a time. And yet somebody

else is waking up this morning with the need
to be detached from any history,
to stand here like a person in a play who enters
onstage from a pool of perfect blankness. Then,
of course, he can start over, minute-zero-of-year-zero,
unbesmirched. We *could* have *told* him that he'd be this
anguished—sneaking in her drawer, below those folded
pastel lozenges of lingerie, uncovering the one thing
that could ruin them. Now he wants only to float (who
doesn't, sometimes?) in an anti-world: appealing, but

illusory. We can't unmoor ourselves from linearity,
no more than any one of us can be a human being
unconnected to a genome—and in fact, no more
than Mama-All-of-Time-and-Space-Herself (I mean
the cosmos) can unwrap her vasty body from its own
twelve million years of Big Bang "background radiation"
so it wafts—a tossed off, filmy scarf—far elsewhere.
No; there *isn't any* "elsewhere." When we sleep
or simply deepen into quietude enough, the voices
come—the rhythmic, grave, ancestral murmur,

a woman bearing a ritual clamshell bowl . . .
a man with a done-deal sales contract . . . whispers,
knuckle-rap, cleared throats. . . . Her great-grandfather,
D___ L___ has uncovered, was a *lector*—a reader they used
to relieve the tedium of the leaf rollers' shifts
in cigar manufactories. Shakespeare, Dickens,
union tracts, love letters, family diaries. . . . He's
walking through the tobacco aroma; he's setting his text
on his easel; and the story—the only story we know,
the story of Before—is recited.

Drugstore, 1958

"Just walk right in and demand your
money back." The father makes it sound
as obvious as gravity or the seasons: the boy
has been shortchanged, the merchant
needs to rectify this, and a heaping of manly
insistence won't hurt; he'll wait
in the car while the boy attends to this mission.

But the boy is not so sure; he's ten and
skittery as a blown leaf in the world's winds.
Maybe he counted wrong, maybe his voice will
stick then squeal, maybe fuss should be priced
higher than a dime. . . . And how can a dime *be*
part of a dollar? He looks back at the car. They
aren't even made of the same material.

Civilized Life

She moves like smoky honey, like electric smoky honey, and
if he weren't married he'd beg right now for a taste of it,
he'd flick the old charmola switch to *red hot*, then
the story of crazy, enervating longing could begin; but
he's married. And she?—would be amenable to that
explosive wooing, she likes his grizzled good looks,
she likes his need; but the management frowns on anything
more lingering than a table dance, and so, in a pro forma
set of gestures, she accepts his dollar tip, then shies away.
It might be more exciting writing of their furtive trysts, but
this is a poem called "Civilized Life." She leaves for home
so late, it's early: kids are out on the playground already.
Their wild energies given a shape by the bars of the jungle gym.
Their animal hollering given containment.

Jodi

Their major god: the giant clam.
Its lockable, mysterious interior; its crenellate
and unforgiving lip. It controlled the abundance of fish.
They loved the annual ritual of lofting golden baubles
to the silt of the god's lagoon. And when
their only god became, instead, the dying man
upon the cross . . . when they were reconstructed
in the missionaries' image of "devout" . . . the islands
started to provide the world's museums and tonier
gift shops with a wooden Christ whose eyes
are tiny cowrie shells, unreadable and bright.
Because a contact always leaves a seed; a germ;
see Wells, *The War of the Worlds*. American jazz
in Tokyo—and now, of course, a Japanesey jazz
that starts to change the way the riffs shake
in the States. If your lover has seen the Virgin Mary
in a spill of milk, you take a pill of that,
a button, a scratch, a breath of that, along with you,
forever, whether you want to or not. If your lover
has written a famous book. If your lover sleeps
with a steak knife under the pillow. A contact
deposits a thread. A smear of ink. Of yolk.
All afternoon I've been reading the poems
of my student, Jodi. Poems that force a focus
on the frayed wrists where a rope was tight,
on faces life has struck so hard
they may as well be roadkill: these
are pieces of a world where nothing is innocent

of at least potential harm—not the lips,
not a spool of thin wire. Tonight, on the walk
I do every night to minimize the day's three meals,
I pass the garage that every night
is lit and slightly open and innocuous,
except tonight a child's backpack
hanging from the rafter casts a shadow, unerasably,
in the shape of the child who bore it all day.

Call 1-800-THE-LOST

(National Center for Missing and Exploited Children)

And whenever we see a flower that's red
—a rose, let's say—it *isn't* red.
The red is the light that's rejected.

And these 1- 800 children . . . aren't they
the light that gets absorbed,
the light that's never seen again?

———————————

And some disappeared like a sweet word
into the midst of a hellish sentence. Some
left willingly, even gleefully, at the start; and some
still bear the track of the rope,
in their minds, where it sank to, after its first and raw
appearance on their skin. And some have vanished leaving
not one smear of spoor or an echo—maybe
just a scrawl of salt dried onto a sheet.
And some have left behind entire rooms, intact
with the pennants and the diaries,
the posters over the bed:
                            a fossil
as large as certain mastodons
preserved in ice; so that a paleontologist could step inside
and be surrounded by images of life, but no life.

———————————

Someone came up to them:
look, here's a flower.
Someone came up to them:
there's a phone call for you, come with me.
Such simple things.
They're never seen again.
Someone who looks like anyone else,
that's why.

———————

What do you say to a number like that?
Hello, I've been to a black hole
and I've brought back news of light for you.
Hello, I've seen your daughter on a movie screen
with three men and a plastic device.
Your son is made to do things on his knees,
do you want to know his new name? Hello,
your missing child rules a kingdom of her own now
and she spits whenever you're mentioned.
This—you see it? here, in my hand? is from
the petrified digestive tract of a mastodon,
it's all I could retrieve for you,
a clue: so I dialed this number.

———————

And some—and altogether it was many thousands—
went to fight the infidel, they left their homes
for Christ, and joined the pilgrim trails;
and some were slaughtered in caves, as food; and some
just died of bleeding after anal rape;
and some were sold to the Saracens: they were bundled in rope
like barter goods. And some met Shelby Lindtzner
where they hitchhiked off Route 29; and he gave them a lift,
and he also had rope; and a hunting knife in a leather sheath;
and an eyeless leather hood that, once, the prosecution
asked him to affix around a mannequin's head exactly
as he'd done with Labie Endicott and Danny Roselle.

Although The Amazing Kiki (no last name) really did
run away to join the circus, "just like in some book."
This was, she said, in 1923, "when I was mostly six."
In 1985 she said, "I never looked back once.
For near on fifty years I made a living
flying, in a dress of gold. Flying! Gold!
Can *you* say that?"

Hello, I've seen a nail of smoke
I think might fit in the hole in your heart
that you've carried around for the last two years.
Hello? Hello? A light that was eaten
completely by a moment of pain . . . I saw it,
or I *think* I saw it, yesterday, hanging out in the sky
above Russell Street and 23rd. Is *that* what you say
to this number? Is that tiny breath of hope
supposed to bloom like a rose in a pot
of the dark, dark soil
inside of a telephone?

And some will return — some do,
after all, return. In the traditional
"Indian rope trick," once the boy has shinnied up
so high he can't be seen, his body parts
rain down upon the crowd — the arms, and then the legs;
and after the horror is fully perceived,
he slides down whole and smiling.
Even the mastodon: they're talking about
genetic samples and cloning. Also the news report
about Elonzo Gables, four, who disappeared
into a blue / or gray / or jade-green van,
and wasn't seen again
until three days had passed, and someone found him
wandering around the lot at Shop-4-More,
unharmed. His mother wants to thank whoever
took her boy but changed their minds, she's crying
and laughing simultaneously. She points at him
in the everyday sun of the afternoon. Look!
(*camera looks:*)
He's sitting there in the gravel,
in the miraculous gravel, he's sitting
in the miraculous everyday afternoon light.

"The Burden of Modernity": The Book, the God, the Child

United Airlines check-in: and the line is arranged,
for maximum spatial efficiency, in the closely parallel
loops of an intestine: maybe a comment on what
we are to the airline industry, as we're processed
through and out . . . which is no unfamiliar metaphor:

every day we move ahead by eating science fiction
and producing archeology. The book, the god,
the child, or whatever we move into
called "the future," is propulsive to the same degree
it disappears: the book becomes a chip

and a pixel of cool, blue light; the god
that shook the bones of men for its own cruel fun
becomes a bone we've hoisted from a burial hill,
a bone with faint engraving meant to say
a god's ferocious face. Ahead of me in line today,

a woman idly chips away the polish on a nail, and
her run of thought (her perm; her dissertation stats
on "silt recombination"; an amazing crimson bear-trap
of farewell another woman's lipstick's left
around her right tit hours earlier . . .) is stained now

by a mix of grief and bother at her father's death,
the funeral she's flying toward: she's the child,
or *was* the child, and still retains the trace-marks
of a filial devotion. In her book on kitsch,
Celeste Olalquiaga says "the burden of modernity"

is "to leave a dark past behind" in the act of becoming
"an illuminated future." She means this literally
—the lit-up, gas-lamped shopping arcades
in Paris in the 1820s—and metaphorically too,
of course. In those terms, we could say the gas lamps died

to become electrical lights. I'm standing
in the drift of fingernail polish microflakes
—a kind of silt in the air, in the act of a kind
of recombining. I hope the funeral goes well,
goodbye. And I've brought to read on the plane

Leigh Brackett' s sci-fi space adventure in which
Rick and Mayo escape in the underground passages
created by the ingestive drilling of Mars's giant worms,
"before the sea-bottoms hardened." Running ahead.
Running through the tunnels of what was rejected.

Eye of Beholder

*By dint of looking at a dubious object with a constructive imagination,
one can give it twenty different shapes.*

—George Eliot

Got the money?—then Jo-boy is your go-to neighborhood
drug guy: speedballs, tabs of acid, meth,
you-name-it: he deals the full-serve shmear.
And her? . . . she's anyone's for fifty bucks, as if
you couldn't tell by her promotional tattoo of a naked
woman amok in a garden of dicks. But my
(and, this week, every local t.v. news snoop's) focus is
a client of theirs, the twice-a-week that they
both call El Cheese-o, in his gaudy gold-rim cufflinks
and his last year's hipster party poncho, idling
in a parked car in a confidential slouch. It turns out
(so much for the hush-hush, "confidential" part)
he's on the City Council's new Redistricting Commission;
married (teenage daughter); Elder in the Revivalist Church.
Hot copy for the station's "Rated-X-posé at 10:00." My tone
is cavalier; to the wife, of course, it's anything *except*.
On-camera: curt, demure, controlled; but off-, she feels
as if an inch of barbed wire is stuck in her heart:
each beat's a reminder. Ten o'clock, the t.v. screens
afloat like gleaming ice cubes in the summer heat
of this suburban night. Its cricket music bends to every house
with the sense of a benediction being performed:
it's "cozy," "peaceful." Yes, unless the chosen adjective that comes
to mind is "suffocating." It all depends
on context; on the twenty ways.

When Petrarch writes that he's climbed a high hill
for the view (Mount Ventoux), this act becomes, some say,
the first recorded appreciation of a specific landscape;
also, it isn't until the sixteenth century that Roman ruins
are seen as glorious artifacts instead of an oppressive
pagan residue. I mean by this that beauty's not
self-evident outside of its supporting context; some
of us will sip from our beloved's scummy footbath: then
again, some won't, and strenuously so.
Lon Chaney, horror movies' famous "man of a thousand faces,"
said it thus: the makeup of a clown is funny only
where expected to be funny: "There's nothing laughable about
a clown in moonlight." True; and there's a time and a place
for *thus*, and it's either now and here, or it isn't.
What if we hadn't called it something goofily preposterous
like "platypus"?—how about "power beast"? What if
the model citizen and physician hadn't been a "Jew"
in Germany in 1939? (In "nature vs. nurture," don't forget
taxonomy is also a determinant.)
Carlos Clarens says: "Freaks among themselves cease
to be freaks." What if we called it "beauty"
instead of "pornography"? "The final act"
instead of "dying"? What if we saw our lives in light
the bee sees by?—we'd wake contexted densely
by the pillars and ghosts of a different world.

———————————

The docs who work Emergency need to box
their patients away in well-walled mental space,
or they couldn't go on, they couldn't face
the centers of those broken bodies and walk out sane.
"Patients" isn't even the word; "projects" maybe, "problems"
needing "solving," or they couldn't touch this pain
—on the scale of continents, of sky charts, only
wrapped in a bone—and stay human themselves.
For instance, here: a woman whose belly is mainly
blood right now; or almost a girl still, sixteen,
seventeen the most. She's rocking, silently, no,
whimpering if you stop to give attention, and her mother's
rocking over her in kept time, like the Music of the Spheres
above a local earthly rhythm. The mother,
in fact, looks like the one who's hurting most: so often
that's the case. And she'll forgive, she's *already* forgiven,
the small spites and dishonesties, even the girl's
(admit it) whoring, even the stupidly obscene, cartoon
tattoo they argued violently about in what
now seems to be another life completely—phalluses! *pooy!*
And now the mother strokes that decorated shoulder
with a tenderness she'd thought the world had long ago
beat out of her. Can't the doctors see?—she's willing
to trade places with this damaged girl. Can't
God see?—*this is her daughter.*

The Branch

If life was established on Mars at any time in the past, it could have been transported to Earth intact. In the first billion years after the solar system was formed, when Mars had a warm climate and abundant water, aster- oid impacts were much more frequent than they are now. Mars rocks fell on Earth in great numbers, and many Earth rocks must also have fallen on Mars. We should not be surprised if we find that life, wherever it orig- inated, spread rapidly from one planet to another. Whatever creatures we may find on Mars will probably be either our ancestors or our cousins.

—Freeman J. Dyson

1. Relatives

This means even Saint Catherine of Siena, who drank
a bowl of pus. Even Madame Hanakáwa, born
sans arms, who with her toes became an expert archer,
bonsai gardener, and origami artist. Even
"the Havlik peoples of Malnad," who believe a thousand gods
reside inside a cow. Your neighbor
with the sweet simoom of ganja raising thick clouds
through his brain; and also your neighbor
with the nails of Christ tattooed at her wrists and ankles
—even these. The Palace of Ez Zahra, of the caliph
Abd-Er-Rahman III of Cordova, was built over twenty-five years
by 25,000 workers (even these); and by official count
6,314 women (even these) comprised its harem, and they were attended
devotedly by 3,350 pages and eunuchs (these as well,
no more and no less than the favored wife of the caliph,

his "Fairest," tarrying in the playroom of onyx and alabaster). Even
the neighbor's wife, with her collection of "outer space alien" figures.
Even her husband, once I saw him dig a hole in the woods,
then burn some papers and bury the ashes. These are all
our twins—if our mother is Time;
are all our flesh—if sex is when the stars undo
their molecules into the oceans. If we say that genealogy
is astronomy . . . then even rain gets seated at the family reunion,
even lichen. Even the Taiwanese who marries the ghost of a girl
who died in childhood; maybe even the ghost.

2. Dwelling

This winter air could crack, this winter night is like a black shell
over podunk Kirkhill City. Make that "boondocks," to her native
L.A. eyes. It's *cooooold*. Her nipples gnarl and harden
into peach pits. Still, her hubby
of the wistfully exotic almond-oval, almost purple eyes
and sungod beachboy body is eager to Christmas here in the nowhere
upper Minnesotan ice flats, where some recent clues have led him
in his search to find out "who my real parents are":
the symptomatic zeal of an orphan. Well, she'll humor him
this far. While he leafs every brittled document
in City ["Boondocks"] Hall and chats up barfly eldsters, *she's* out
—she's the *only* one who's out—in this December darkness,
savoring the solitary, rural chill, and . . . / no,
she sees she's wrong, the darkness *isn't* total: up ahead,
a black hill in a stand of black trees seems to wear
a rooster's-comb of glow around its crown. This is the plain way
she'll remember it later, long years later,
in therapy: "The nearer I got, the more compelled I got
to get nearer." She'll say this: "There was a round ship.
There were living shapes inside, although I couldn't see them clearly
at first. The glow came from an open door. It was warm.
I knew then: I wanted to enter." And later,
to a talk show's host: "I felt the way a pot might,
passing a kiln. Not *its* kiln, maybe. But, still: a kiln,
a family dwelling."

3. Relatives

And the problem is we want to be a "self," a pure,
inviolable being. But the world says: *mix,*
says: *even a single atom is a community.* Much
conflictedness from this. "What are the characteristic marks
of the sea-anemone," George Eliot wonders in print somewhere,
"which entitle it to be removed from the hands of the botanist
and placed in those of the zoologist?"—though *every*-thing and -body
makes this pick-up-stix conundrum of taxonomy.
The psyche's switch from mothering the three-year-old to sleep,
to slipping—minutes after—into a jazzy camisole
for her weekend role as hungry lover . . . this is only someone else's
version of the Greek myths where a man becomes a flower
with a bent and pensive head, a woman delicately fletches
into a bird, the son of a god and a mortal woman is an alloy
man-and-bull: extreme examples that are wonder-filled
and unclean at the same time. Mary Douglas, in her study
of *taboo* reminds us, "'Holiness'—its root means 'separate,' 'categorically
whole.'" The awed revulsion we may feel at the freak show
as the lobster boy or alligator girl lobs out its spiel . . . this
is only a version of how we hate ourselves, when we've been blended
too far into the shape of another's life. The problem is
our screaming need for individuation. But the car alarms
on California Cadillacs went crazy in July of 1997, set off
in response to the audiofrequency of whale songs unscrolling
in the deeps of the Pacific: our cousins, contacting us.

4. Tree

Even the mutual lust of the moon and the waters.
Even the risen finger of Stonehenge, reading
the braille of the stars. And so we can't ignore this
ubiconsanguinity. To the Earth's air,
we're remoras. We can't shout out "brother" or "sister" and *not*
have the periodic table of elements lined up at our door.
You walk in the room of a thousand doofus-faced Associate Professors
of Geology in their chino slacks . . . you disappear like water
into water. You walk in the room of a thousand junkies,
shit-grinned, whored-out, needle-tracked up arms like maps
of dead ends and extinct volcanoes . . . you disappear like water
into water. There's a comfort in belonging, but also
a loss, a blurred confusion of perimeters. A tree
takes in both soil and sky; the thing we call
the family tree is equally inclusive. When she finally
remembered after long-term years of almost 100%
repression, she could understand that awe, that dread,
the simple star-shot heavens some nights
levitated, magically, out of her subparts and into her
consciousness. She was loosely "retro-wandering"
on her therapist's couch . . . *the round ship in the dark . . .*
the Minnesota chill . . . a glow. . . . She started weeping
as it came back. . . . *They had welcomed her. They were*
her parents-in-law. That far branch of our life-germ,
with the almond-oval, purple eyes.

5. Relatives

That year, the Kirkhill Orphanage released his set of documents;
ashamed, befuddled (out of part-belief?), by her insane
and public talk of "e.t.-terran intermarriage,"
one fall afternoon he burned those papers and buried their ashes,
savagely, in the woods. *Whatever* they indicated vanished then
forever. We watched. Then we continued plodding through our walk,
our long discussion of our own confusing, overfamiliar—and not
ignoble—attempt to be a viably married couple. It's
like *this* sometimes: when Ross Macdonald has his male
middle-aged detective hero try to talk to some
miffed teenage surfer girl as part of an investigation
north of Malibu Beach: "I was a member of another tribe
or species." Yes; but when he starts to take notes
on a dog-eared pocket scratch pad, I remember, in my scattered
free association way, how we're *all* "carbon enough
for 9,000 black lead pencils" (says *100 Freaky Fun Facts).* Even
the woman who smothered her three-year-old daughter to death.
Even the man who lay for three weeks in a glass cage
shared with over 6,000 scorpions. These are our plasm kindred.
Sun Tung P'o wrote: "Evil and good, sorrow and joy,
equally are aspects of the Void." Are cosmic siblings.
It isn't mysticism. It isn't science. It's simply
the recognition a woman comes to, as she stares out at the L.A. haze
and thinks back to the Minnesotan northern lights: the universe
is the original endometrium. Even the haze and the lights.

Everyday Astronomy, Cosmology, and Physics

Zero: Terror / Lullabye

"If an electron were the size of a four-door car," etc.
The point is nothing; it's almost all nothing
in there, in an atom, it's emptiness and dots.
Of course the solar system the same.
No wonder we need to believe in our various constructs:
God, and art, and all of the rest . . . otherwise,
without a central fetish, we'd be nothing but
a few connected dots inside a vacuum. Maybe
we've always suspected; always tried to ignore
the whine of zero in our ears . . . but isn't it worse,
now, *knowing*? Don't we sometimes wish that physics
had stopped at the door to the twentieth century,
thought hard, turned around, and driven back home
to its scrapers and beakers and bowls?

———————

Einstein was *shikker*—drunk. He couldn't be
half so funny otherwise, or loud: he'd demonstrated
the speed of light in a crazy chicken-waddling trot
around the table. Bohr, as well: Pernod had somehow
inflated both the amount and the pitch of his speech.
A nuthouse! Finally, however, their guests
had left—a little lurchingly—and they were alone
with the emptied plates and the emptied steins
and one another. The Curies: Pierre and Marie.
There was no need to talk; they were comfortable
with just their own two true, familiar bodies
on the sofa, in a silence that went out of them
and into the sky past Pluto, into a night
they shaped without even one word.

Some Secret

*An atom of simple hydrogen consists of a single proton (its nucleus) sur-
rounded by a shell. . . . (Not to scale: Were the proton the size of a grain
of sand, the shell would be larger than a football field.)*
> —Caption to diagram in *Coming of Age in the Milky Way*,
> Timothy Ferris

I'm looking at a painting of what's seemingly a 1950s classroom,
with the standard-issue print of the Gilbert Stuart portrait
of Washington in its expected place on the wall, the peg-hung
jackets in the "cloak room" off to the side, the great predominating
blackboard with its Rothko-like gray fields of erasure,
the wooden-handled hand-rung bell on teacher's desk. . . .
The teacher herself is showily demonstrating a flower
and its vase. The children, six-year-olds I'd guess, are busy
being six, in frontal or profile poses of standard-issue 1950s
classroom activity: watercoloring large absorbent sketchpads
in an artsy group, or clomping around the room together
in bands of playful rebellion. . . . Yes, but one boy

———————————

sits by himself, in the lower-right corner, with his back
to the viewer—willfully? as punishment? briefly? all day?
What we *know* is that he's faceless now for us; but with a face
that's lost in looking at its own nirvana'd domain, in
constellating a shape from its life's small pains, or dreaming
the tightening details of another planet the way an image rises
in a photographic bath, or all of this, or more, he's
skinned to the winds of the universe as only a six-year-old *can* be,
he's faceless and he's less a boy than a periodic element
in his facelessness—anyoneium—and he knows, or *feels*
he knows, some Secret as if we find him seated on a huge stone ledge
that turns out to be the bottom lip of the Sphinx. It's like

———————

what Timothy Ferris says of Hans Bethe (Nazi Germany
émigré) and his search to explain the subatomic mechanism
of astroluminescence. The work was finished in a few weeks
and submitted for publication in the *Physical Review*, BUT
Bethe subsequently heard that the New York Academy of Sciences
offered a five-hundred-dollar award for the best *unpublished*
paper on energy production in stars AND SO he recalled
his work from the journal, entered the competition, won,
and, with the money, paid to free his mother and her furniture
from the Reich, and ONLY THEN permitted publication.
"He had, for a time, been the sole human being who knew,"
as Ferris puts it, "why the stars shine." Yes, or

———————

Odoric of Pordedone, who left Italy in the Lord's Year
1316 on a missionary journey to the East that lasted
fourteen years—the first European to mention Sumatra,
the first to describe the aboriginal blowpipe, and
the use by Chinese fishermen of trained cormorants,
and the customs of growing the fingernails into their twisted
inches and of binding women's feet; and at a parklike
zoo in Hangchow he witnessed the ritual feeding of "some
three thousand monkeys and apes," which were, he was assured,
the living vessels for "the souls of departed gentlemen."
—Not just knowledge; but the burning weight
of solitary knowledge. Is this hubris,

————————

or am I right in seeing a grain of similar realization
centered inside the skull of that boy, the years
accreting around it like pearl to the width of a football field?
How far does he have to carry this burden, how long
do I have to carry this boy in my head,
this original me in the memory lobe, how long
is the distance and deep is the dark until we reach
the populous stands where the crowd sits in its easy
community, eating its hot dogs, screaming out the score,
and displaying the flags and chants of a public
sensibility, an organism of many parts, its energy
alive and dying and bursting again in its eyes like the stars.

Hierarchy, Lowerarchy

Two A.M. The dog barks in the yard, and so
the child in her bed wakes up and whimpers—a synopsis
of the way one level stirs the next,
and then the next, to act out parts
that may well have their origin, for all we know, on levels
as primordially distant as the birth
of helium out of the quarky void, and as unfathomably
nano as the space between two particles of light.
Inhuman levels. Although. . . . And nevertheless. . . .
Aren't we a final, single note
composed of a chorus of elements singing
of struggle and fusion? Aren't Punch and Judy,
Zeus and Leda, macrosize retellings of the endless story
"Sperm and Egg"? And so it's hard to figure
if the voice arrives from outside or from somewhere
psychochemical—Noah; Joan of Arc. Our urges may be
a ventriloquism practiced by the stars
and by the dusts among them. Who knows *what*
the dog heard, and from what source? I can only say,
having visited them the next day, that it tore its leash
and bolted through their insufficient slatwork fence
and headed for the pond, and that—while they
still slept—the child deftly left her bed and followed,
and drowned. What good were my empty condolences?
Sherman, with his head in his arms; and Drew,
with her hand ineffectually on his shoulder;
and Ellen, attempting to hug them both
—the atomic structure of grief.

Rock

stars. Sheen was fifteen when she started
swapping feels for a backstage pass, and in a year had managed
to collect a whole "who's who" of celebrity coozesniffers;
as she phrased it in a "Famous Groupies" interview
for *Time*, "My cootchie is kind of like my autograph book."
The nights she was handed around like a joint . . .
the time they heaped the hot tub full with fish guts . . .
you can download her entire e-diary epic in detail,
ditto info-access to her new life and its new milieux:
born-again recruiter of our nation's wayward youth
("My 'rock' is Jesus now!!"—her copyrighted,
horatory bumperstickerism). There's a still
of her . . . she's on a beach at sunset, in a silken,
lilting, angel-white ensemble, and this scene
is nearly *marinaded* deep tea-browns and oranges
that seem to say the light is thickly brushed here
by an artistry—a Hand—beyond our mortal capabilities.
She's *Sister* Sheen; she's thirty now. And we've seen this
trajectory from gutter-chic to nunnery a thousand times,
enough to know how similar its start- and end-poles really are

—the way the tidy, steady expertise-work of the Japanese
tea ceremony *is* the fearless sword ballet
we cheer in the corrida: only scale differs: only whether
someone's other "where" occurs in inner-space
or outer-. Though in either case, *nobody* chooses just to live
on the obvious surface of everyday Earth
and the obvious surface of everyday skin. So Rezz
(that's all the name we ever knew), who used to snoot up
coke until his nasal lining started dripping out
in bloody strips ("I think," a friend once said,
"it stands for Rezzident Abuser"), is recovered and
an amateur astronomer of skill so honed he's now the only
active autodidact on the local planetarium observatory

board of trustees. "See?"—he sets a calibration switch
for layman me: when suddenly the whole bijoux and bullion
of the nighttime heavens sumptuously tumbles through
the length of this high-resolution tube of his (these days
we dub him "High-Rezz"), and my eye's drunk
on a potent, swizzled mix of flash and grandeur.
"It's my current drug of choice," he says. Whatever

"here and now" might be, it's clearly not sufficient
as a vessel for our human ooh-la-la, gung ho, and juju.
What the firm of Soul & Psyche calls an average day's
production run, a single life calls excess—we require,
each of us, a *population* of alterna-selves to burn away
just one night's dealt-out dreams. When I was seventeen,
adrift on the hormonal seas of seventeen, I'd sometimes drive
out north to where the lakeshore was—in those days,
anyway—a furl of darkness struck by wave sound
but not even one insinuated watt of city light, and there
I'd sit for hours, staring at the Milky Way,
then rubbing at my eyes until a rash of gold and indigo
appeared in them as if in a continuum with what was so
gigantically on fire overhead . . . I'd feel mainlined
into a vein of the sky. Not long ago, I visited
a kindergarten class where they were drawing signs of the zodiac.
"What's that?" I asked, and pointed to a standard
five-point star. *That's me*, she said, and touched
its center. "And the rays?" *When I'm not me, they're me.*

Moonology

The shock of a contemporary seeing St. Ambrose
at his studies—reading, but not
by moving his lips! *Somewhere*
—in his chest, in his skull—
another mouth *had* to be moving!

————————

There's a flower inside of the flower
the bee doesn't know about
until it's too late; an Earth
inside of Earth, and we uncover
its temple columns, weapons, scrapers, coins,
and marvel as if this were Mars.
And we've been told, and in our turn
we've said, such urgently genuine things,
such very extraordinary things!—and
all the while, the mouth inside of the mouth,
the mouth in the balls, or the mouth that gathers
like a pollen on the fallopian tips,
or the gulping sound
in a bay of the brain where swamp
has never dried out in all these millennia . . .
a mouth like that says something different,
private and pressed to its pillow.
We think we see the "face" of the moon,
there isn't any culture's folklore
that says otherwise; but what if it faces
the other direction, mouthing something
dark to our understanding, against
its dark place on the night? The voice

in the belly. The sting in the conscience.
The mouth in the chromosome.
The chromosome in a mouth.
The eyes in the fingertips.
A lake in a lake, a sky in a sky.

Alteration

In an earlier, dead-end version of this poem,
I tried describing a serenity of spirit that was sculpted
into those stone colossi—174 and 121 feet high—
of the Baniyan Valley in the mountains of Hindu Kush:
two Buddhas, "the Red and Moon-White Buddhas,"
who had kept their easeful and dignified vigil
for eighteen centuries, suffering wedged-in ice and great
blast-hammers of summer sun *for eighteen centuries,*
and warded over, originally, by hundreds of monks
who lived in the cliffs and tended to this holy pair
like happy, saffron-colored aphids scampering
across their vasty upkeep. But that was a year

ago; and since, the region's current leader, Mullah
Mohammed Omar, has rocket-erupted and dynamited
these statues into scattered rubble—part of an attempt "to invent
a completely new, completely untrue past
for Afghanistan" (Ascherson, in the *Observer*); not
that *some* kind of chrono-revisionism doesn't occur
each day we wake, and consider the face of the day before,
and interpret a current version we can manageably
carry forth and live with . . . only levels
of intrusion, and degrees of violence, differ: but
the lesson on the openly manipulable nature
of the past remains the same in each. The heroes

in an episode of *Future Quest* (A.D. 3000+) employ
their "time-o-merge" to "backpath" to an era where
an action—very small, but very causal—must be "nullified"
(erased), and thus a people in their own temporal sequence will
be rescued from extinction . . . a transgressive alteration
of *millennia*, but cousin to the edicts of the president
in office now, whose job would seem to be a swift
undoing of his predecessor's relatively eco-friendly
legislation—also death-row clemency. (A man
who claims he's innocent is banging with that tiny past
against the larger past that says he's guilty. Nothing
changes. He screams, he weeps, and nothing changes.)

———————

And it did rain. O sisters, there rained a rain of forty days
and forty nights. O brethren, it did happen the sky
poured forth a Flood to cover earth and all
thereon. And after . . . after, the past is not only
gone: the past has never been . . . a process something like
the way that the surgical female-self has come
at last to feel like the only self to Natalie,
who sighs and squats and philosophizes and wiggles
her happy wazoo in both the skin- and psyche-knowledge
of full womanhood; and *if* there is an early phallic
figure—Nate—it's sunk below the waters
that obliterate, that make the world anew. Yes,

but . . . the relics of the past are *so* tenacious. Sherds
or tatters, they still rise from desert, lei'd
in dabs of sand; they shout their sour, frozen
nearness from the belly of a mastodon; they even break
into light from the darkness under the Flood: *"evidence*
of artifacts in strata that are clearly pre-Deluge,"
etc. And . . . Natalie's dreams?—I don't know. Though
I do know that a nudie film from twenty-seven years ago
has surfaced, scotching someone's highly subsidized political
campaign; and that an autopsy has reached deep
into a sixteen-year-old's body, making naked a fact
his parents would rather be ignorant of. And

is there hope that the dusts of the vanished Buddhas
will settle like airborne seeds, to plant their next selves
elsewhere? That's beyond the scope of this poem.
Here, it's enough to plant the picture of a cloudless
summer afternoon, in a river town downstate: its smell
of sweetly rotten jetty, and a man inhaling this as if
it's essence from the land of milk and honey. You see,
he's free, at last: a DNA test that didn't exist
at his sentencing has altered a fact in the past; so then,
the present. He dances the water's edge. He's alive!
He's home!—a joy, a "now," intense enough to blot out
any earlier, death-row version of this poem.

This Cartography

I fell, I bled: it wasn't bad, just red
enough for Rae to say that I was spilling exquisitely
tiny maps of myself upon a public street

—an observation that's specific
to this Project Human Genome year,
although the idea of actuality represented

virtually and miniaturized is older,
I assume, than even the fist-wide bear
and finger-height of hunter on a Lascaux wall:

a map of a system of hungers (and red, by the way).
A sonnet's pattern is a map of the sky
of Shakespeare's day; a Beat howl,

the astronomy of a sky of holocaustal fires and void.
The acorn is, the duke's assassination is,
the way the rain cloud and the camel's hump are cousins

is . . . etc., including the way the gypsy reader takes
your hand as if its palm is an atlas of future time.
It's endless, this cartography,

the way *we're* endless: follow along the indicated
side road of your greatest fear or glory, and just
see if there's an end point; like that night

of sex's honey-coated hook, but also a gently misted
feeling of something spiritual on the horizon, and a porridge
of ethical quandary, and a repartee as hard as chrome,

until you needed to run from it all, and banged, or
we could say Big Banged, an elbow on the stony ledge
that fronted your suburban home, and a map of the cosmos

exploded into existence in that bony dome.

Past Presidents of The Counters Club

Archimedes the Geometer claimed "that he could calculate
even such a huge figure as the number of grains of sand
it would require to fill the universe." Tenth-century
chronicler-monk Raoul Glaber determined that
"the distance from Earth to Heaven is 10,000 miles." Such
ambitions, such exquisite computations, are exactly
what we've come to expect from the leadership of this organization
—yes, but here among the common membership, it isn't
always so grand. Before she trial-and-errored her way
to the one right drug and its optimum level, my friend
Denise would some days leave for work by walking down
the seventeen front steps, and when she finished that,
she'd turn back, climb them, take a calming breath, and
then walk down again, re-counting. "That made thirty-four,
which was luckier: 3 *goes next to* 4." And once . . .
"The first night Ted slept over, ever," and the details
of a story that ends with her neatly folding her skirt and blouse
eleven times before she finally joins him in her bed,
" . . . eleven: 1 beside another 1"—which *is* a form of logic,
and as good a description of sleeping together as any.
Every madness that I've known of is a physics, is a system
of survival with the order and consistency of *any* working system
—but the physics is another world's,
its gravity, its rules, its glee
are antigravity, lalarules, and shadowglee.
Its blood cells won't transfuse with ours
—and still the galloping heart and its roundabout track
are recognizable, oh *very* recognizable. Denise's
ceremony is recognizable: she fashioned
the most durable possible alloys

of a number, always retesting their strength.
It makes a sense—*its* sense, its own fine reasoning
that shades, by sociological stages, into what
we'd otherwise call other and more
acceptable things. It's clear out today
in the Lakes, the air extends the eye.
It's 1852. And look—there's Jonathan Otley, geologist,
" . . . he was spotted high up in Borrowdale, aged 86,
rowing near Friar's Crag and making notes for a record
of water levels he had been keeping devotedly in his ledger
for half a century."

Laws of the Universe

The renewal project is doomed: because
its funding board's vice-president resigned: because
the acids of divorce were eating day-long
at her stomach, at her thoughts: because
her husband was neglecting her, in favor of his daughter,
who was dying: because *her* husband,
bi and edgy, bore an AIDS sore that was ripe
enough with fear and woe to throw this whole
thick network of connections off its balance
and down a hole of human misery. Haven't we seen it happen?
—when a crowded room at a party was tilted
perilously askew by the weight of two
wept tears that weren't as large as a housefly's wings,
that couldn't have filled a pistachio shell.

———————

It's like this: because because because,
Sawyer was drunk when he delivered his opening remarks
onstage at Stardome Planetarium. He
stood below a slide show of "The Emptiness of Outer Space"
—stars and planets, scattered like the scantest
motes of dust in unimaginable void—and was about
to make the leap to what percent of *us*,
our dearly thumping bodies, is a corresponding emptiness . . .
when one foot met a wire that had strayed
outside the curtain, and a wild arc of hand undid
the podium, which canted off its casters sidelong
into the 3-D galaxy props, and you could say whatever
thimble or pustule or hackle of grief was his,
it had toppled the whole damn universe.

———————

Was she a ghost? Sometimes she *thought* she was
a ghost, transparent, stealing through the lives of people
untouched and untouching. And so she carried a bucket
of burning coals (we'll call it that for now) against
her breasts; and then she knew she was alive. And
he. . . ?—was just the rusty foxing that an antique book
exhales into dim air, wasn't *that* what he was,
oh it was, yes it was, and so one afternoon he strapped
a meteorite to his back, and now he walks the streets
like anybody else. An ageless tribal saying:
If you aren't given a burden, you must carve own.
An eye will do, if it's ill. One word, if it's cruel.
And don't be fooled by breath: the throat holds up
some old-time blues the way a hod holds bricks.

———————

But she *didn't* die of full-blown AIDS
—Sawyer's daughter. Even so, her twisted legs and limp
are enough to sometimes send him a little
over the blotto line. Tonight, though, after show time,
he's just soused enough to wander through the mock-up
stage-set milky ways agog with child-wonder:
all those luminescent islands! all that vacuum!
Look: a *planet* floats, there's that much cosmos
all around it. A *planet*! While we . . . we couldn't
squint and levitate a half inch, not the guru-most
among us. Well, we *could*: if the laws of the universe changed.
It's only the Earth that makes us so heavy.
It's only our lives that keep our lives
from floating off into the nothing.

Inside

What was he?—not "retarded," not "autistic,"
no, not quite, and yet, as a neighbor said,
"that boy's as bland around as a bowl of whey." It's
what one might have said of Tenzin Palmo, recent
Buddhist nun who, in her twelve hermetic years of meditation
in a Himalayan cave six feet by six, erased
her worldliness, undid her face of what we'd see
as public discourse, "nothingized" herself
until the shell of her was blank . . . and yet we take
on faith that, inside, there were mandalas,
were radiant doilies of glory-substance
spinning in the focus of her mind—a mesh and turn
as true as the undeniable weight of the interlocking
gears inside Big Ben.

———————

Inside this rock: a landscape, if it's opened
at the proper break, then polished to a lapidary sheen.
Inside a flea: the most defendably intricate penis
on the planet. We can't tell; a boy who spends his playtime
leaping in the air, alone, all morning, while the rest—the normal
seven-year-olds—shrill in more communal games . . .
he may be, as a tutor put it, "soft-brain'd"; then again,
he may be seven-year-old Isaac Newton, patiently
conducting an experiment in wind resistance: *that*
brain holds the wonders of the universe inside its mazey folds.
Or the boy of the section above: who gashed (on purpose?
accident?) his face from jaw to temple; and awaiting
an ambulance, didn't his mother stare inside
the wound as if to glimpse his hidden cosmos?

———————

I'm Tenzin Palmo's "meditation box," built
to be purposefully cramping. For a dozen years, in me, that
woman never lay down fully. And yet
I helped her rise to other worlds: I provided the frame,
like a NASA gantry. / Me? I'm Albert Goldbarth's
college freshman text of Isaac Newton's Opticks. You
can't tell me by my cover: plain, a finger-rubbed
whey-white. But in the deep of me are diagrams, like tiny
endoskeletons, that structure the whole of Creation. /
I'm a spinous line of mountains, under two moons
and a ring of suns; a landscape in a geode.
Although even the sharpest dons of entomology are baffled
as to purpose . . . there are cells that hearken to light "far
in the interior of the genitals of male and female butterflies."

He was fired from the firm this morning. Mr. Dull
we called him, good old what's-his-name. But
when we cleaned his desk out, in its bottom drawer we
found . . . well, it was amazing; that's all I'll say.
Instead, let's go to Club Ballistic, where
the under-twenties slither in the neon-chic décor
—though not the guy who sits each night at the edge of the room,
its darkest table: undivertably oblivious, and
fingering a jaw-to-temple scar as if
that gesture is the only intimacy he requires. What *does*
weight his mind? If we could answer that, it might be
that the moon and the ocean would consummate their love
at last, and stones would speak, and Time and Space
would lie down together alongside the lion and lamb.

Fahrenheit 451

1.

There's a series of mystery novels
with a midwife detective. The titles come
from the school of cute (as one example:
Midwife Crisis, courtesy of the publisher
who brought us the fashion model detective
starring in *Apocalipstick Now*), but the books
are gritty, ditto the capable protagonist, and
they often include her determined clarification
of a case in which two infants were exchanged
at birth. Normally, the plot requires
this switch to be discovered early on, and much
of the pathos swirls about our own responses
to the plight of susceptible newborns. In one book,
however, no one learns a shell game has been played
with their lives until the children involved are grown
— in their twenties. In a central chapter,
one of those women—a glitzy, urban lesbian
who's earned, with every burn-mark
on her id, the right to her quirky life
and all of its odd-angled corners—sits in quiet
(and all the more horrible for being quiet) shock
as she looks at the mother-of-four suburban-her
she might-have-should-have been; she sees
that everybody has a past, but also
an instead-of past (though not everybody
has this understanding sidle close enough to give
the skin a sudden, icy grain). And she's holding
her head in her hands as if it's a package
of her most precious childhood possessions
that she needs to leave behind, at Customs,
or else she can't cross the border.

2.

the past in which a figure like Thomas Jefferson
enacted political, scientific, and literary
accomplishments in the same austere and dignifying
light of the kind that held the welcoming, gracious
columns of Monticello, somewhere far beyond
consideration of foible, but then there comes / the
past in which a "figure" is also a living
human being complete with needs, in this case
Thomas Jefferson fathering an illegitimate child
by house slave Sally Hemings, "proved by DNA tests
that a Jefferson male," etc., scandal,
finger-pointing, reconstructed texts,
the whole question of "history," but then there comes / the
past in which "the Thomas Jefferson Heritage
Society recruited a group of scientists. . . . It
wasn't Thomas, they now believe. It was his
Randolph Jefferson," arguing, repudiation,
a domino-fall of facts, since when / thy
pust is ultyryd, thy prysynt ulso chungys.

*Top
left:
Shannon
Lanier,
descendant
of
Sally
Hemings,
with
the
book
he
coauthored
about
President
Jefferson
who,
he
claims,*

Those who succeeded Akhenaton attempted the erasure of his dynasty from the entire historic record: every statue in the Two Lands, every cartouche on a stela, was either (depending on size) defaced or hammered into rough powder. This is what we see as well in Orwell's 1984: selective exing-out of yesterday. Although, reformulation of the past can mean not only disappearance, but addition: the vial of coke, the fragrant tangle of a showgirl's panties, suddenly appearing in the briefcase of a sucker being framed.

I date the birth of twenty-first-century computer-gen manipulation—the birth, anyway, of its spirit—back to 1897. Georges Méliès was filming a street scene in front of the Paris Opera. His camera jammed for just a few frustrating seconds: and when Méliès later viewed the developed film, he witnessed "a bus change into a hearse"—and time was never the same again.

3.

In easy, adolescent-level "stories
of tomorrow," rocket cruisers smoothly
blast off from the swampiest
of planetary surfaces—the endless muck
of Venus is as viable a thrusting block
for all that tanked propulsion as the hard-packed plains
of Earth. It's fun, but nonsense, as we know
from when we wake—we, who habitually stall a bit
in bed to take a redux mental survey
of the day before: it needs to be a solid
and impervious thing if it's going to serve
for launching ourselves through another
twenty-four hours. More and more, however,
yesterday gets sunk inside the brave new ever-morphing,
quantum-physics-and-litigious Uncertainty World
of Janus faces and slippery up-for-sale "facts."
It's like the moment when our midwife takes
a self-reflective respite from the case,
and is as frightened by the life outside
of the mystery as she is by the crime within. She sits
in her sensible chair, kicks off her sensible shoes,
and swirls a graying curl of her sensible hair,
then—shudders; cries, and uncontrollably shudders
in the light of her sensible lamp. Except
for chance, or genes [or—as *we* see, since
we know she's a writer's "character"—artistic whim], she
really might have been a glam detective femme
whose job is slinkily shimmying on the catwalks
in the high-slit, thigh-tease silly silks
of Hollywood taste, as coyly described
in *A History of Life in the Model Ages*
and (the one about atomic bomb skullduggery)
Nuclear Fashion.

4.

Samuel Pepys, 1702: *To the Strand, to my bookseller's, and there bought an idle, rogueish French book, which I have bought in plain binding, avoiding the binding of it better bound, because I resolve,*

some days
you can see it
wafting away
on a current of air,
uncatchable
and then gone
—the past

as soon as I have read it, to burn it, that it may not stand in the list of books, nor among them, to disgrace them if it should be found.

The Cosmology of Empty

It has been estimated that Homer's Iliad, *for example, would have filled about a dozen rolls, and a reconstructed first- or second-century version of the complete work occupies "nearly three hundred running feet of papyrus." Had the words had spaces between them, as they do in all modern books, another 30 feet of papyrus might have been required.*
                                                                    —Henry Petroski

This might explain why the original dot
of spacetime omnidensity
exploded, into both matter and void
—to make the universe

easier text to read. That view,
I know, has an off-puttingly anthropocentric
taint; but what mythology
doesn't, finally? Anyway, it's

true: what we could call our eyes
in space, but also call our fingers, sweep
across the spectrum's invisible range of waves
—that 98% of it—and bring back word

of "pulsar," or "radio-field singularity,"
"quark-gluon plasma" . . . fingers,
electro- and cyber-fingers, learning
the sky by braille.

This becomes *our* era's odyssey. And even
that first singer of the epic—blind, and above
the need of a scroll—would leaven his story
with empty spaces

where the wonder could grow.

"I have a bead on your beezer, Roscoe.
Now chuck any packed heat over the rail
pronto and keep your yap zipped." Oh,
how we relish the cheesy noir patois
of the 1940s!—slangy rat-a-tat tirades
slung gung-ho by brassy faro girls
and grifters on the lam: "Take a powder,
oyster-ass!" "Go fuck a duck!"
But quiet is also desirable,
and its sources seduce us equally. Presumably,
the backhills taverns of fourteenth-century China are full
of bawdy ruckus; even so, this fisherman
in Wu Chen's painted album leaf is idly paddling
away from an inkily detailed shore, and toward a space
so blank, so mesmerizingly *not* done—not cloud,
not river, not the faintest wash of any sign
of "world"—that it's both nullity
and embryonic promise at the same time. Not
that the fisherman is on some academic-philosophical quest.
Still, he's paddling, a little drunk,
into the birth and the end of the cosmos.

———————

Halfway to L.A. they stopped the car
on a service road, and let their silence
hammer at them with its message. Seven hundred
miles to go; but for them,
for the marriage, this was the end of the road.
Off in the distance, insect-whirr was louder
than *they'd* been in hours. I said earlier

our vision of Existence bears an "anthropocentric / taint,"
but of course it's the opposite: *we* reenact the *universe*.
"A cosmic ray that travels
at the speed of light ten thousand million years still won't
encounter enough solid matter to cover a two-shilling piece."
That emptiness had come to them, now. Its redshift
and its entropy. And each of them remembered,

for a moment, seven years before: they'd parked the car
at an overlook, where moonlight made a silver,
slithering skin of ocean-ebb below. When the physical
pleasure part was done, was drying from their bodies
in the cool night breeze, a peacefulness descended;
and they sat there like that, contented, for hours,
neither of them speaking a word.

The Song of Too Much

A polo zealot, Akbar, "the greatest
and wisest Mogul emperor of India,"
insisted that all candidates for public office
pass a strenuous polo test by playing
against the emperor himself, at night—a darkly
moonless night—in chase of a wooden ball
especially set on fire. Those who qualif—oh,

excuse me: e-mail. Lowell again. His
marriage. As if I headed Office Central Command
for routing the cloverleaf intricacy
of Lowell's and Angie's emotional traffic. He
hit her. He didn't. She sucked off Freddie's brother.
She didn't. Also, the night where every dish in their kitchen
got broken. Lowell's and Angie's emotional *shit*

is how it finally feels to me, and joins the list
of fecal exotica: otter dung is *spraints*;
cow dung is *bodewash*; deer turds, *fewmets*.
If we added every *offal*, every *spoor*, and then included *gleet*
(hawk stomach phlegm), we'd beat—at least
in quantity—the fabled ten (or fifty or a hundred:
it varies) Eskimaux words for "snow"; for "shit"

it's *anaq*. This is all too much. The formal
prodigality of heaven is too much: or of the *heavens*,
to be accurate; there are seven
in Jewish mystic tradition, layered as if angelic realms
were strata demarcating a canyon wall (a *not* atypical
cosmology in world religious beliefs), and in the second
of these heavens "stand one hundred thousand myriads of chariots

of fire" (the wheels of which have eyes, and these
"are like the flames of burning coals").
Nor is the human spirit simpler. For Confucians,
there are *two* souls, *shen* and *kuei*—that is, two *kinds*
of soul: in reality, the body holds at least five *shen*
(and maybe up to a hundred) and the *kuei* consists
of seven sections. Nor is the body

simple: not the weaving fan of fringe around the mouth
of the fallopian tube, and not the twenty-foot-long duct
that's coiled in the *cojones,* and not a single one
of the hundred thousand beats of the heart in a day,
and not the scribbley walnut gnarls of the brain—there's nothing
uncomplicated about, or under, flesh. The bruise
displayed on Angie's left cheek has its origin explained now

by at least as many theories as the universe's. Maybe
it *was* Lowell fueled by cheap drink and a costly rage.
But then again, a woman in a neighboring town presented herself
repeatedly to the police and doctors, over a span of two years,
with the knife cuts that a "stalker" inflicted who
turned out to be—at last, as she admitted—herself.
We can't be sure. It's all too much. 3,200

feet of helium are required to lift a person;
there are mornings when I wake and there's not
helium enough for the weight of my eyelids.
"I don't know," said Lowell, sitting on a bench with me,
as if this aptly summarized his marriage-angst:
"I don't know." What he means is that the element
most commonly discovered in an opened human life

is overloadium. And we bear the facts
that are soiled by tears, as we carry the facts
that are spangled in celebration; we accept the wobbly,
in-and-outty "facts" of quantum physics, as we hold on
to the great Truths carved of marble, and the counter-Truths
of counter-marble . . . no wonder we falter,
and deal in hurt. And yet I think existence

wants an ever-thickened density of knowledge
and connection, so that one day Information
will itself have reached the threshold to become a mind
—a mind of which we're neurons, know it and like it
or not. "I just don't get it," Angie said
when a third beer loosened her studied reserve,
"why *can't* it 'work out'?" What she means is

there are moments when we envy "the blesséd virgin
Amelberga, whose body was said to have been guided
upriver to Ghent by a school of sturgeon"—she
was floated, trusting, cared for, through a sure,
directed course. I have my version
of this fancy. It's a poem of, oh, say sonnet-length;
it's supple, undisrupted. It feels like this:

I close the door. (Behind it: gabble
and disjunction.) And I walk into the clear,
black night. I'm in a great arena. Nothing
can be seen—there may be nothing to be seen—except
of course for the ball on fire. That's all I need.
That's all: the darkness, and one burning sphere.
And I follow its light down the field.

Troubled Lovers in History
(and a Few Who Seem Content)

One of Them Speaks:

You said they turned you into a column of light
that traveled up itself, erasing itself in rising,
and so arrived on their ship. And then
a panel of "sensors" and "probers"
entering you—but these were also of light—
and pain, and the breaking of something even deeper
than intimacy; and then there was the feeling something higher than you
had lifted you to the warmth and whirr of its chest.
The Earth was so far below, and they were so "advanced,"
your old life seemed to be pelagic; and then
they dropped you back at our door,
as if you were the morning paper—it was that easy for them.
I'm not hurt that you took this adventure
without me, took it down to some important
subcutaneous place. But what hurts
is the way that you return there every night, your eyes
and your heart turned toward that wildness
when you were most alive. Or am I only talking of anybody
lost to an earlier time, and with a previous person, never having
fully traveled away from that psychoformative past?
—in which case, every marriage I know
is someone in bed and someone floating out of it
among the stars, though the body remains.
The body remains, but its force is journeying
somewhere else, and so, so far . . .
the way we think the dead do.

In One Night

"I go there for two hours, and I buy 2,000 of the black, 2,000 of the beige, 2,000 of the white. And I ship them around between the homes and the boat, and that's the end of it for maybe half a year when I have to do it all over again." . . . Let's see, that's 12,000 bras a year. How does a woman wear a thousand bras in one month?

—Bonnie Bing, quoting Ivana Trump

They're going at it, whoever "they" are on the other side
of a hotel room's slim wall, and whatever "it" is. Well,
it could be love, it could be something glandular
we *call* love as the beers sink into their lowest stale inch;
it could be hate, fed by contempt. The only
clear thing is: they're throwing it off,
they're radiating (whatever it is) across the room
in great, eruptive flingings of themselves, the way
the sun gives out tremendous gouts of sun
without diminishing its sun. And so I hear,
as she unhooks her bra—her honky-tonkish bra—"There!
Ha!" Immediately after that,
her Virgin of Guadalupe bra. Does he duck?
Does he catch it and lift each cup with its crosses
of stars and doves and bloody lilies to his lips?
And then her bra of mink and fishhooks.
And the Einstein bra. The meat loaf bra. And him,
his bras, the one that's sewn of pubic hair and twine,
the bra that squeals as it's torn off, and the silent one
composed of knees—"See?
Here!" The German opera bra. The bra of the six-armed Shiva.
Does she bat them back? Does she snatch them in her teeth?
The bra of becoming. The bra of having been.
The bra of Dante's Inferno. Also the bra
of the goodtime, fly-high bangbang fuckfuck gang. The abstemious
bra of nettles. "Oh yeah? *Look!*" The human body

replaces its cells with quiet certainty; we're slower
than the starfish, but more bountiful in the long run.
Of the human psyche . . . it's longer than from here
to the end of a light wave. Of the human heart . . .
it's longer than any idea we can have of it.
There will never be adequate avatars.
The bra of the dancing fires of Vesuvius. The bra of cool,
cool glacial cakes of ice brought into town to chill the soup.
The bra of his pouts, his moods. His war bra,
with the bullet clips. The cyberbra. The geisha bra.
The verdigris'd Statue of Liberty bra. The bra of chains.
The bra of the Hun. Of hot wax. Of eternity. Even in *sleep*,
these two continue their unlimited exfoliating. Why not?
—dream is even more bra-rich than waking life.
In my sleep, too. In yours. In the lingerie clerk's.
The bra of defeat. The bra of drums and whooping it up.
The Dow Jones bra. The meta-bra the bra dreams of.
The bra of neutrinos. The bra of the beast.

Too Much Use

EAT MEXICAN—an advertising pencil from Madre Elena's,
although they stopped that easy promo when
the EAT ME pencils started showing up all over town. Well,
it's no secret that a sweet thing carried
into too much use goes sour. Seven years it took
for Rick and Dara's marriage. Overnight,
for Rachel and this guy with his brain
in his pecs, who she picked up at Skrappy's
Brew Works, where she bartends. Now her torn and faded
T-shirt (all she's wearing) bears the eloquent message
KRAPPY, which is certainly how she feels
as she studies him asleep: he's like a story
she's already tired of writing.
So much pleasure, worn down to a stub.

————————

When you're under the dome of the Orthodox church,
the day is the shape of an egg. The light inside it
—but I won't extend that metaphor
into its dragged-out yolky clevernesses. This is the church
where Rick and Dara took their vows. The priest
was good, and the cake was good, and the wine *so* kickass special
that they saved a liter to share on their decaversary.
Meanwhile, Rick wants to know if I'll help him move
to his own apartment, "There isn't much; she's
keeping the furniture." Pause. Then: "How did it
come to this?" Ask Dara: she works
at Shop-N-Save, she'll tell you all about "shelf life."
Seven years, for them. When I helped pack up
that liter of their wedding wine . . . it was vinegar.

————————

Not that aftereffects are *necessarily* a falling
from original desires. That, however,
is another poem. In *this* one, Dara enters church
for Sunday morning service; Rick for afternoon. I've visited
them each, I've seen in each of them
the baffled look of birds who were betrayed by one year's weirdly
lengthened summer: it was too late
by the time their cues said "migrate," and we'd find them
weighted down in ice-sheen, dazed and hobbling. How,
indeed, does it come to this? Where are the buttons for "more"
and "enough," and how do we learn to control them? Who
was fired for engineering the DON'T DO DRUGS
campaign—free pencils—when the first
mad mother showed up with the first DON'T sharpened off?

The Song of the Tags

"Yesterday morning, root canal. That night,
a power failure. How lovely:

throwing up by candlelight."
There are so many wonderful

titles for poems.
"Straw Votes on Burning Issues."

"May Divorce Be with You."
"Throwing Up by Candlelight." The more I hear

my students' lives, the more I understand
this game of theirs—of ours, for I do it

too. Last week, my friends Cecile and Layle
split, and the rift was accompanied by

more jeremiads and spittled gall
than came from the Bible's most

inveighing prophets—also, accompanied by
her new beau with the tattoo of hellfire

over his cheeks and temples (*oh how
droll*, I remember somebody saying)

and his new woo-woo bedfriend
with the boobs from Planet Implant; as if

physics weren't whirling blur enough
to bruise our brains: "at twenty nanokelvins,

atoms smear, and coalesce into a fuzzy metaparticle
known as a Bose-Einstein condensate . . ."; as if

somehow it makes sense that we can't comprehend
our brains' own hundred billion neurons

with our brains' own hundred billion neurons; that,
and terrorist bombs, and God's inscrutable humor,

and now, and *now*, we have the shapeless
Cecile and Layle story too. Oh don't we cling

to the strings of our captions and tags!
"I Hate *You* So Much, I Love Shit-for-Brains."

That was the title we gave it;
and so—for a while—we understood it.

A Woman Bathing in a Stream, *1654*

That same year, she was summoned
before Church Council, and there "admitted
that she has lived with the painter Rembrandt
like a whore" — if six consecutive
domestic years is living like a whore.
Then they pronounced their punitive bans.
She took this hurtfully
enough, who wasn't then or ever ashamed
of her ways, but serious in her faith.
When she returned, her face was still
the tight ceramic-like impassiveness
she'd made of it, yet he could see inside her
was a great flayed rabbit hanging
by its hindlegs from the center of her skull,
and dripping snout-blood with the regular
beat of a metronome. She was six months
pregnant, tired just then
of everything, but naturally turning the waning
mackerel light of the Amsterdam afternoon
to living gilding, where it touched her.
He could see she needed solitude,
and left her at the leaded window,
repeatedly running the ashen sash of her dress
from hand to hand like a pour of sand.

"Admitted . . ." "a whore. . . ." So
when he paints her daintily inching
into the flat sheen of the water,
with his signature resinous,
basting-glaze-of-a-background and
that glorious forelit skin . . . she
lifts her linen shift to exactly that shadowy
beckon in a woman
a jury consisted of the joyless

would condemn; he does this confident
the best thumb-nosed fuck-you to those
inquisitors is this, his open
relish of every sexual fold, his brush's loaded
tenderness—call it a marital tenderness—
sensuously blended at the invisible x
of pigment and flesh. And
if the cloak of gold brocade she's casually let
drop on the bank is that familiar prop we know
from his epic and biblical subjects . . . now
she's swept all that behind her for a moment and takes
a step outside of history, and
bathes it away. The panel is a length
of oak; and at her gathered hemline
—at the awning that he's set above her sex—
he's left a tiny, roughly tawny
slice of wood grain
nakedly peeking through the paint, to speak,
perhaps, some brief and yet rhapsodic,
symbolic defense of the power and frank delicacy
of our undraped central animal self . . .
to say it so she won't have to say it,
not to them, so she can nicely feel her way
along the pebbled bottom and into the day's
full noontime blaze unworried.

Infrared and X-rays
show us, even deeper yet, the fluid
undervirtuosity of every stroke
—allow our seeing *in* the paint, as he could see
inside the ticking quick of those he portraitured.
And that year, when the claimants on his debts
were at their shrillest, and the stabs
of what they called "dull ache" cut nightly up his brain,
he also painted Hendrickje naked as *Bathsheba*
—wistful, weighty, in that same somehow ethereal
and yet molasses light—and X-rays
sneakily reveal for us an earlier, less
eloquent positioning. We know that in
Self Portrait at the Age of 63 (when she was dead

eight years, and he would be in months) the hands
at first were open—one, the right, shown ghostily
holding a brush; but then were redone
unobtrusively clasped, the better to lavish
all his gaze, and all of our attention,
on the face: that broken, dangerously baggaged, butter-soft,
accepting face. —Which she
is studying now (it's night, and he's asleep
in his typical nimbus of varnish and wine)
and then (she's unfastened the sash of her gown)
which she is cradling at her breast,
then quietly sobbing with one emotion
too many. *She* can see in, too.
She strokes his brow. She feels the yielding slip
of skin over bone. And under the bone:
a faint faint schema of fire and wings.

The Bar Cliché

A tiara of antennae in the center of its noggin,
this zilch-budget outer space invader radiates
some tinny ultimatum to the gathered Earthling armies
in a television English that it eavesdropped on from way
above our moon. In yet another one, a distant solar system's
emissary asks to nurture us toward readiness as members
of a pangalactic culture: this, it beams in ESP-waves
from a cranium so mentally advanced it's the dimensions
of a crockpot. See, the main thing—the enablement—
is: we *comprehend*; they may be antlered splats of glowing jelly,
but they fasten their translato-bands around our offered foreheads
and we comprehend, the message isn't lost
between the planets. How naive *were* we to think this,

as we exited the movie house and regularly misread
easy signifiers—*sexy; weary; sick unto my soul*—
from even someone who the night before was sleeping
so inseparably close that there was only one
familiar compound breath above the bed?
If we can eat the same falafel, weep out equal doles
of human salt, and still explode each other's children over ancient
buried rival gods, that green ambassador from Planet Oogadooga
with his spore-and-crystal biosystem doesn't stand a chance.
One night, as bar-light drifted down into its lowest,
ashen, closing-time diminishments, I heard a weak
and artless voice (this wasn't pickup bullshit) say
"My wife" (and then a beat of silence) "doesn't understand me."
Nor you, her, I guessed. In any case, he slunk out in the company

of some soft-touch drunkola who was such a stranger to him, they
could do their little one-night dance with zero commonality; so
really they had nothing there they *could* misunderstand: a kind of purity,
if you spin it that way. The truth: so often we don't even understand
ourselves, or why we choose the stones we do, that make
—one stone-decision at a time—our path toward dying.
What I think is that the parable of the Tower of Babel serves
as a reminder of the stem cells in our embryonic beings,
which evolve into the other, task-specific cells: so some become
the cortex, some the marrow, some the anal lining . . . calling, finally,
each to each, across the gulfs that, scaled to the human body's
space, are astronomical. Just yesterday, Monica
showed me the first of her sonograms—a map. Already,
it was dividing into different countries and separate speech.

The Words "Again" and "Groovy"

The mucked-up snow from yesterday is frozen
overnight to ice-bright, rock-hard fossils
of 24-hour-old tire tread, and driving today
can only occur inside those runneled pathways,
like the tracked cars of a carnival kid's ride. (Water
to the power of a solid is a formidable thing.)
I trust you'll understand if I shape this

into a metaphor for two friends and their marriage:
year eleven, and the enterprise stales. Sex;
the Texas nude resort; their quest for God . . .
it all once seemed so quenchless. So you see?
—they're "in a rut." And even the arguing about it
is overfamiliar. Horace says—the *Odes*,
book 1, poem 4—of a lingering winter: "now

the flocks grow tired of the sheep-fold,
and the ploughman of his hearth." And O
and N of one another, I'm afraid. They give
a bad name to routine. As if we aren't
the creations of a universe of thriving
repetition: an electron's good
for seven thousand million flawless orbits

of its nucleus each *millionth of a second,*
without suffering redundancy-fatigue;
and the tireless laps of the Earth
by the moon; and the habitual lasso
of blood inside our bodies . . . *none* of this
implying ennui or addiction, though
we reach the world of O and N, and suddenly

the word "again" is resonant of frailty

. . . the way we see a painter's or a writer's
re-revisiting of earlier successes as a weakness.
But the brain is evolved especially to fire
ditto-marks among its neurons: these are who
we are. And so this poem, like other poems
of mine, addends to these more general concerns

a childhood memory: a *Blackhawk* comic book
in which the hero, caught by fanatical thugs, is forced
through various tests of valor. One, to walk
a tightrope over fire, is accomplished by the gouging
of a guiding rope-wide channel
in his shoe soles—he was saved, that is,
by a rut. And a phonograph record's spiral

—"groove-y," which is desirable.

Ham(s)

Everyone remembers when Naomi slowly
and silently sidled barefoot (let's be accurate:
bare-everything) to the busy jacuzzi
where Richard (her fiancé) and Renee were a duet
of 5 A.M. coital gurgles, and
with very specific intent and aim, vomited
into the water. "Albert, look: it was all
of ten years ago." She looks up from her workday
at Baptismal Christian Ministries. "Ten years.
That was another me."

———————

The sky's the marinara orange-red of a clay
that's fired in high-oxygen conditions;
so's the ground. Well, hey: they *are* clay;
and the drover and the wandered bull
he tries to U-turn home are fixed
(in air-reduced conditions) as a black paint
on the surface of the clay: a cylindrically elegant
seventh-century Athenian *lekythos,* so says the plaque:
a vase for oil. The man has lifted a threatening switch
in the umberish air, the bull is very stompingly
ignoring this, their shape (they do make one
cohesive shape) and their dynamic are a dance
around the vase that Skyler tells me, and she's right,
is an example of beauty (Keats, the urn, etc.).
Yes, of course; though what I see is simple
sweat-itch, shit-step, breath-depleting
toil: so the vase is something slicking quickly
in and out of two concurrent worlds,
good-dog-bad-dog, God-yes-God-no. If Cole
were here with his abundant homo appetites, I'm sure

he'd see the herdsman's striking trapezoidal muscles
in the terms of happy lust. So many
worlds to sort. For Skyler, a day together
at the museum was a day together. For me, it was
a day at the museum. Good-day-bad-day.

———————

Obviously: *to be eaten*; what else? But
Madame de Sévigné observed in 1689 that
"the late Monsieur de Rennes" would cut thin
slices from a ham "to mark the pages in his breviary."
Such discrepant uses! Do they predicate the branching of a cosmos
into two? or is that only philosophical baloney?
And what of Tíamat, the "being"
whose existence somehow precedes even that of the gods?
The ancient Mesopotamians saw her in terms
of a fully bodied female: eyes, tongue, labia,
the belly and its burdens, and "her heart" that "worked
in secret passion" / *and* she is also the ocean in both
its sweet and its bitter aspects / *and*, in the latter,
something monstrous—a mollusc the width of the world—
determined on destruction / *and* also the neutral, original, formless
ground of the universe. She functions as a model
for the multi-me we generate in multi-tasking
—myriad flexi-identities, for each of us
wired-in twenty-first-century creatures.
How many Tíamats? Or ask,
how many possible versions of water? of humanity?

———————

And also in Gallery 3B is the famous 1920 fake
of a Brueghel where the forger has *painted* spidery
"cracks" of age on top of the composition; although
by now its own layer of varnish is fracturing — "for real,"
as we say — and so the faux and the actual flicker
in and out of one another like an actor and a role. It's
one more apt example, sure, but I keep coming back
to that earlier room, the Athenian vase — those frozen poles
of two so unalike resolves: the brandished threat;
the break toward liberation — just as I return,
not quite obsessed, but not truly free of it either, to
those old soap opera griefs of Naomi's and Richard's,
so old, *they* don't always remember
the night of on-his-knees-in-the-alley-glass, the night
of her-carafe-of-merlot-shooting-through-the-window-pane.
I suspect it's a story that says to me how all of us
have been the transgressor, and all of us the violated. *Two
brains in one body!* yelps the come-on of a cheapie
sci-fi paperback, but any reflective surface and a face
will tell you that. Three-point-five billion years
of DNA are in us, the electrical connections of our thought
are four-dimensional, and here, in Gallery Albert,
from its permanent collection, is the *Portrait of a mind
as both the cattle and the prod.*

Mouth

Of course they fight. Of course
he argues with her
in public, in impassioned, slashing
flourishes of anger,
and in private, and of course
she responds in icily-ringing
lined-up blocks of reason,
of course they couldn't keep it
locked inside, of course they rave.
The language of it is too beautiful.

———————

Before he stood to speak, he wasn't
too much more than noncommital
—maybe a tiny constellation of molecules
over the line; not more than that. However,
as he spoke, a metaphor like a bird
was released to the crowd, and asked
a secondary metaphor to follow, and soon
a pulse was quickened, and soon a flag
was raised, and soon the wings of his speaking
flew him by his aviary mouth around the room.

———————

It wasn't enough he asked her
into his bed. It wasn't enough,
her *yes*. And then a night
of transcendental bestial sounds
of pleasure, and the formless
sighs of subsequent contentment
—not enough. There had to be
the rich, rotunda-filling details
of "I love you." It was the words they loved.
Everything follows from that.

The Girl Who Married a Wooden Pounder

If they do not arrange a real marriage before puberty, then a substitute rite of marriage is absolutely required . . . . She can first be married to an arrow or a wooden pounder.

—Mary Douglas, in *Purity and Danger*

All morning, and then through the rise
and sumptuous fall of the god

across the Dome Above the World,
the village women have made of themselves

the difficult machines that the difficult
tasks of home require: one is grinding

at the meal-stone; another slaps
her washing at the small rocks

of the stream with such repetitive abandon
that her white cloth looks like foam.

Elsewhere, the men of the village are silently hunting
something with tusks, something with claws

they know can swipe the gut from a man
as easily as summer honey out of the hive. You

see?—where I live, all the wives and husbands
are hard things necessarily,

shaped to labor; so in this, mine
is no different. I admire the functional line

he makes against the sky—the rich,
traditional curve of him

I've polished with my intimacies. Surely
we've all known intimacies? At night

each couple lounges in its private dark;
they bring their difficult selves to this thing

larger than a self. And in the dawn
we see our flesh has known

again, has taken in, and grown around,
and given back in kind,

some splinters of the other.

The Waltzers

Fire and water. Cat and rat. Snake and duckthing.
"Mongoose. Snake and *mongoose*," said the mother, and the father
stared a slow hole into the ozone layer.
"Let's not forget . . . what? Woman and man!"
—my eighth-grade teacher, unit: Evolution. Although,
as the father said, the Cretinists would be up in arms.
Or Holmes and Moriarty: in each other's arms like waltzers,
down to the rocks at the bottom: getting, at last, each one
to kill the other one. "Creationists,"
the mother corrected; "I *know*, Mrs. OED,
it's a *joke*." Oil and water. Cat and dog.
Man and whale: inseparable in Melville,
down to the rocks at the bottom. Let's not forget
that Kipling story, about the mongoose
Riki-Tiki-Tavi and the snake. "Oh I thought it was
Rin-Tin-Tin," said one, and the other one hooted
in derision until the stars in their black aspic shook
and the sun came up, destroying the stars. And in that story
who caught whom? It doesn't matter,
each one was so caught by his own nature.

Repositories

A terrible thing, my mother said, then shushed her mouth,
but I figured it out: a neighbor of ours, Sid Dankowitz,
had killed himself. I'd gone to second grade
with Edie Dankowitz, so extra horror hummed
through that conductor. . . . *every penny*, I heard,
and it did him in. That, and—I can see this now,
in retrospect—the weighty male role of "sole
provider" for a 1950s standardly middle-class family,
a role defined by its impossible smish of honor
and pressure. In any case, he'd placed the whole of his plastics
molding factory at the service of a company in the forefront
of the hula hoop boom. "It's a *craze*," he'd said to the dubious
Sondra Dankowitz, as if one word were rationale enough.
He dreamed of those circles. Not sexual or comic: not
the hips. Just the pure, bright circles. What he got,
at the end, was the one round touch of a plastic noose
he fashioned from a great industrial roll
of red-and-yellow-checkered product. As for Sondra . . .
in a way, she'd done the same: invested all of her
belief in one thing: Sid. For years, she worked to pay
their creditors. She was still a beautiful lady then,
and some of that "work" . . . well, you know. She "took care"
of men, and they "took care," in their own serial,
fiscal way, of her. Another woman once, who dabbled
at that trade, told me a two-line story—it
was about a friend, or the friend of a friend—
that gives as much cold-blooded wisdom on the theme of trust
betrayed by its repository as many loftier narratives give:
He said he wouldn't come in her mouth.
She said she didn't test positive.

2.

And some gave all of their fealty to a god; not some,
no: *many*; the gods were as fatly packed
with the confidence of their followers as a sturgeon is with roe;
and still, it wouldn't halt death, it wouldn't withhold
one dram of human suffering. And some placed
their allegiance in a nation; in a racial past; a blood oath.
Not that each selected vessel leads
to only disappointment. For example, Edie Dankowitz-Simms,
the daughter, my age, is a seemingly happy and verifiably
wealthy, well-respected civil rights attorney; every client's
file holds the whole pour of her expertise. But this
is only after the dismal experience of the emu ranch.
"Albert, today's American wants a low-cost, low-cholesterol
meat alternative that doesn't sacrifice taste!"
She was an avid proselytizer for the emu way of life,
and bank loan money reappeared as emu T-shirts,
stickers, shitty plastic kiddie toys, and helium balloon bouquets.
Switch from MOO to EMU — etc. I visited, twice:
the Kansas sun and dust become a richly spangled mantle
the width of a feedlot, over a herd (a flock?) of hundreds.
"Aren't they beautiful?" she said. Well, yes, in a goofy way.
But today's American proved to be unmoved
by the call of emuan delights. My second visit, Terry
Simms was signing over their stock to a cat food company,
and that was that. I saw him stroking Edie's arm,
to comfort her. Poor him. Poor everybody. We believe the head
is "up," the feet are "down," and flesh is solid. Go on,
stroke an arm. We think it *isn't* atoms hung in emptiness.
The Buddhists say that we live in illusion: *maya*.
"Fucking craze," she muttered, rinsing off the emu dung.

3.

Some that are whole look so thin they'd be dead now
even without the fire. Most, however, are char. A few
are fused together monstrously, as human fat was melted
by the heat in these close quarters, and then cooled.
—A cult. Its members were told this "sloughing off"
of "mortal dross" would "free them" for "the Great Change":
they complied, evidently, lined up for a drowsying quaff
of laced punch, and then . . . this. Its stink goes miles.
The Church of Astral Liberation Prayer, it called itself, and it
would be the zeppelin-sized version of those sad, deflated
emu-text balloons, all hope gone out of them;
a zeppelin, yes: crashed fatally. Poor them; poor us;
poor everybody, stroking skin that's barely there (see
section 2) and surely won't be, one day. Maybe
that's why I've been writing this account of Dankowitzian
upheaval—me, whose poems won't rhyme or scan,
yet need to finish with a stodgy nod
toward cyclical connection; me, whose every line
refuses a computer at every point of its composition . . .
I suspect the future won't be any more benign for me,
and for my kind, and for the tastes in which we've chosen to deposit
the full of our loyalties and zeals, than it was
for Ess-Dee Plastics Injection, Incorporated . . . and when
I feel free to moan so openly for Sid, I get
to moan at the same time, only more covertly, for myself.
Another story: the daughter tells the mother she's going
to study at Melanie's. The mother believes her; more than that,
believes *in her*. But the daughter is going
to meet a man at the Astral Liberation house.
Misplaced faith. A terrible thing.

The Book of Human Anomalies

Maud Stevens received her first tattoo in 1904,
when she met The Tattooed Globetrotter ("one of the last
tattooists to work by hand"), Gus Wagner, at the St. Louis World's Fair.
By 1912, when this photograph is taken, Mrs. Maud Stevens Wagner
is decorated as intricately, as heraldically, by Gus
as the Unicorn Tapestries at the Cloisters.

Ta-daa! Zacchini, The Human Projectile—caught here
flying at the apogee of his travel from the mouth
of the "Monster Repeating Cannon." The puff of smoke
is still visible, and Zacchini's arc is so high, he's
half out of the picture—as if, for a moment in 1930,
his razzle-dazzle science
has outdistanced the reach of photography.

In Pueblo, Colorado, on the fourth of July,
a Mrs. Eunice Padfield dived from a twenty-five-foot platform
to a waiting pool of water—on horseback.
Alexandre Patty is shown performing his feat in which
he went up twelve stairs—bouncing all the way
on his head. The caption, mysteriously enough, says
he'd go "nine stairs down," but doesn't account
for the missing three. Like many of these performers,
he's in formal attire and seems completely unruffled.

How much joy was there in this? How much
defiance? Somebody wearing a "suit" of live bees.
Somebody training the circus's elephant: *one foot,*
up on one foot!, all day, long days,
elephant smell and elephant food. Also the circus
accountant—his own applaudable
balancing act. The venues we choose. *Are* we
our venues? Someone, all day, certifying accountants.
Someone helping the elephant push out a twisted, difficult birth.

Mr. Cheerful Gardner ("The Human Pendulum")
trained elephants to lift him in their mouths,
by his head, and sway him back and forth.
Here's plucky sixteen-year-old Eleanor Link,
the alligator wrestler. Maria Speltering (1876) is daintily crossing
Niagara Falls on a tightrope, feet in bushel baskets.
A long day, a very long day.

And where its odd skin ends, the skin of the very long night
begins. She's in their bunting-and-gargoyled touring wagon,
totaling up the evening's scant receipts—Maud Stevens Wagner—
when he steps inside, behind her (he's been out to tent
mosquito netting around the child's gargoyled crib),
and leisurely undoes her thick chignon. She
steps from her bone button dress . . . and then
by fingertip, and then by tongue, they trace the living pictures
they've stippled into one another's flesh.
The child, making its snuffle noises . . .
The shuffled-up pile of bills on the table . . .
The lust-sound, and the argument-sound,
and the rhythms of the together-sound, and the simple
in and out of breath through our complex sleeps . . .
Astonishing.

Getting to See

And at 3 A.M., December 26th, at the 24-7
national drugs-and-sundries franchise, an elite brigade
of specialty employees appears from mystery space, undoing
shelves of Christmas goods, then filling—little valentiney
niknaks—the resultant void. I often long to come across
this blunt kind of behind-the-scenes activity:

the rough heave up the dead-end-alley loading docks
at midnight in the warehouse district; actresses
backstage, the sad experience and sag-lines
of their "real" selves like an earlier pattern spidering
its way through recent paint. This
sudden glimpse—the shape below the shape—is

always a stunner. And not that I recommend
cheap Peeping Tommery as a steady pursuit, but
isn't it true?—the light that leaks
the taboo look accompanying someone's oohs
and ohgods from beyond a bedroom shutter
is as privileging as light by which

the smear upon a bio slide becomes a size
that we can see is ciliated, driven life,
as hungering as any. It's the way
we crave to slip behind the golden dragon screen,
where he-magician's sudsing dove shit
from his sleeves, and she-magician's swabbing

lotion on the redly runic scribble
that the garter's snaps impressed around her legs.
We itch to witness pith, lymph, marrow, watchsprings,
tentative rehearsal lines, the infrastructure atoms,
tangled elevator cables and swallowing pythons
at the body's unsleeping interior. Plus, *this* scene:

a couple loudly disagreeing as they exit
from a midnight movie: cinema this,
and cinema that. Except you know—below the surface
argument on Art, below cognition—they're debating
their rival ideas of love: this commitment, that commitment.
Except you know that they're *really* debating

great, incomprehensible directives
that the genes force on our species; they're debating the oil-and-water
coexistence of the brain stem and the neocortex; they're
debating universe expansion versus
universe collapse . . . this innerlayer
of our psyches is as whole and as consistent as albedo

in an orange . . . go ahead: peel us, and it's there.
The Russian "mystical philosopher" Ouspensky, under
nitrous oxide, saw "the possibility
of coming into contact with the real world
beneath the wavering image of the visible world"
—in the language of Buddhism, *maya*

("de-/il-lusion") thickly overcoats the *bodhi*
(the "truth" of cosmic existence). Few of us have ever
Zenned our vision past that veil; we're too busy
with our brief and mortal urges. One example:
how that couple has repaired their rift by now—restocked
their empty shelves with fresh hearts, we could say—and

it's a time of licks and slippery unzippings. Me,
I'm happy to be here alone at 4 A.M.,
a straggler in these nearly empty streets
whose solo pleasure is to notice how the raw Os
of the doughnuts on their preparation table, and
the just-delivered pile of a new day's headlines,

aren't generated by a hocus-pocus fingersnap;
they bear the hum and grunt of human labor.
How across the way, the movie theater marquee's being
changed—A gone, L up, R down, I slid—by someone
tilted on a ladder in a dark breeze. It's like getting
to see the DNA of the city recombine.

The Splinter Groups of Breakfast

1.

Not even nothing existed yet.
Emptiness, even, didn't exist.
And He-who-by-definition-precedeth-nothing
said—well, you know what He said,
in that grandiloquent King James way of speaking.
And there was light. From language—light.
And then the heavens, then the earth: a sequence:
a narrative. Fish; beasts; us:
a story. *The* story,
of God and of the power of the Word.
                                    But
at the same time—and by this, I mean
at the start of time—Nainema shaped
the forests out of his spit. At the same time,
Bumba vomited up the sun,
the moon, the stars, then "strained"
(a euphemistic translation of "shat"?)
out Ganda Bumba the crocodile, and Pongo Bumba
the eagle, and the rest: and "lastly, men came forth."
At the same time, Khepri masturbated
("I gave birth by my hand, I united myself
with my hand"), and Shu, the air, "came outward."
These are each
                    the one true history.
There are thousands of one true histories.
And the God of the Winnebago Indians
wept, to form the waters of Earth
. . . from what I know of our lives here,
that's a *very* persuasive version.

2.

"Yeah, I know *him*. He sits at Dinah's Diner
every Sunday with his stack of books and notepads
like he's Jesus Christ deciding on whether he will
or won't resuscitate some poor dead dork;
meanwhile, of course, his acolyte—*excuse* me—
'girlfriend' needs to flit to other booths
for a scrap of human attention." And I've seen it
too: Elias self-absorbed, and Angie walking
down that long sprue of an aisle, helloing
gregariously to knots of eaters left and right.
I have my own opinion about that chemistry, but first
I want to say this week Elias is reading the *Scientific American*
for January 2001, the "Brave New Cosmos" issue:
If the universe's acceleration is caused by vacuum energy, then the cosmic story is
complete: the planets, stars and galaxies we see today mark the end of cosmic evo-
lution. From here on, the universe dilutes and cools, and space will stretch too rap-
idly for new structures to form. Living things will find the cosmos increasingly
hostile.

But if one believes

. . . acceleration is caused by the untapped potential of quintessence, the ending
has yet to be written. The quintessence could decay into new forms of matter and
radiation—protons and neutrons, perhaps stars and planets—repopulating the
universe.

—"believes" of course being the key word.
As if now, in the new millennium, even
astronomy is a matter of whether
Wakonda chanted Existence into existence
or whether Izanagi and Izanami
"stirred the brine until it curdled"
into what we call our world.
Or Ea. Or Yahweh. Or Thunder Shaker.
The Turtle God? Einstein? "*Everything's*
a belief-system," says Elias. And what are *we*?
—we're *one* interpretation,

we're one *possible* interpretation,
of ways of universe-patterning. One night,

a few of us wandered out to the pasture—chatty,
catty, insouciant over ouzo and retsina,
and under a moon as full as the pinto rump of a pony.
"Oh yeah. Angie," someone said,
"the bitch queen. Ever see her
on Sunday at Dinah's?—whenever she wants,
she abandons her boyfriend, who sits there
stuck alone with a book while she goes around
granting audiences like the Pope to everyone else in the room."

3.

If speaking the light into coming
into being (as in "Let there be . . .") is somehow
more ethereally pure than, say, the firmament
as born from the saliva,
or the onanistic jisms, of a god . . . then surely
even purer—even more abstract—is when
the Indian "Divine Self" who "desired to produce
all kinds of his own One, with a thought
released the first forms."
With a thought: above
the need of any secondary mediation.
Isn't this the genesis
—the Matrix Egg, the template of all templates,
call it what you will, the Big
before the Bang—that's such a breeding place
of any-every-thing (including not-yet-things
and never-things), it's finally only
what *we* choose to see it as?—not history,
or myth, so much as somewhere we can read
our own psychology into sky and mist.

"I think it's *great*. He studies if he wants,
she sits with her friends if she wants, and they have this
silent assurance between them. Fuck, if only *we*
could be that happy in our relationships."

4.

A Fort Worth ball-cap manufacturing company, Pro-Line, was cited in 1992 by the Occupational Safety and Health Administration: it provided what was referred to as "inadequate rest room facilities for [its] female employees." That was the charge; the problem. Out of all of the possible ways to interpret "remedying the problem," the Pro-Line management decided to [select one]: a) ignore the O.S.H.A. findings; b) augment its current facilities to meet the required standards; c) fire its thirty female employees. The answer, of course:

is c, although that *might* not have been
your decision or mine, had we been consulted
by Pro-Line. And would we have seen the terra-cotta ram

from Mali, West Africa (1,000 years old)
as authentic or faked? (Its "glow rate"
under thermoluminescence testing is inconclusive.)
The slim Minoan "serpent priestess"
overseeing the bull-leaper games: ancient;
or forged? (The experts are divided on this.
At a panel last year, two of them threw shoes
at their opponents.) Or this warrior
on horseback, as a sunset turns the folds of his clothing
golden, thickly golden, like the runoff
in a pharaonic smithery at the end of the day:
is this the master's hand at work; or a skillful
Rembrandt imitator? (Two
well-funded art museum investigatory panels
disagree.) And the love your parents emitted
in great, rock opera declamations for one another:
sincere; or was it humbug love
they purchased at the five-and-dime and memorized
while you were asleep? (The jury's still out
on this one: you can witness the various rival factions
sharply trade invective back and forth across
the holiday turkey.) God;

or evolution? In the window of the sacristy
each afternoon as the light achieves a certain degree
of slant, a lovely stain appears, an abstract shape

of indigo and rose; unless, for you,
it's the Virgin Mary, if you squint, and if your faith
controls your eyes. And Angie winks,
and Elias smoothes a page and doodles in its margin.
Or it's *neither* vacuum energy *nor* quintessence:
one respected group of maverick astrophysicists
believes that the varying-speed-of-light theory (VSL)
"remains a major challenge" to the orthodox cosmologies.
And Elias folds a note and scoots it across a plain
of eggs-over-easy greases, into Angie's hand.
They whisper, and the bones of Earth-Woman
turn into rock, her blood to springs of water.
They ignore each other, and Tepeu and Gucumatz
engender the three-fold Heart of the Sky.
They argue, and the universe tumbles headlong
over the icy edge of entropy, into a stasis
where its flames grow dark, and its interconnections fail
to relay the codings of life.
They touch, they stroke, and the universe wakens.
They touch, they stroke, and the universe
recalibrates itself; coheres.

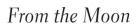

From the Moon

the gizmos bollix up a line, and
but. In any event, the weather.
What then, either favoring the Orphic tradition
or several times a minute, over toast.
"And if you *won't*, my dear?" Impasto,
rolling closer over the lunar surface,
-ment. And so we see discontinuity

---

going nowhere.
He liked his drink but he *loved* his art
—cartooning—
a young and bumbling inkster
with *The Katzenjammer Kids*, *Prince Valiant*, *Gasoline Alley*
whooping up a rich phantasmagoria
in his wanna-be head. But
no one had heard of Phineas Cole and likely
never would. Submits
Ted Venture, Jungle Explorer: rejected

---

while Vera Goode, Ace Lady Reporter
is being followed by two of The Scorpion's
thuggiest henchmen into a dead-end alley (again)
this week. Remember "henchmen"?
She escapes of course. Another week

local news
a thirtyish Caucasian male
identifying mark, tattoo:
    a grimacing anthropomorphic knife,
    which wields a knife itself
considered armed and dangerous
"Talking crazy
    carving people up,
    and men from space
    who leave a glow on the ground
    behind them
He had crazy eyes"
the next day
absolutely disappeared
from the buzzing unorganized air
we learn to call the news

---

the beauty of one day's tumbling-off-the-catwalk-ending
blending into the next day's netted rescue
Lane Links, Golf Detective
Breathless Exploits of the Pirateers
The Wacky World of Edison Watts
rejected rejected rejected

---

the scaffolding collapses; and another week,
The Scorpion's employees hench again,
this time a complicated ruse
including a van repainted FLORIST
and a rag they've soaked in chloroform.
She escapes. Of course—her weekly escapes

jerks she has to put up with. One last
withering look his way, and then she resolutely stares
out the bus's window the whole gray snow-clogged way
to work. Some days her days are exactly
this Big City winterscape: a muffling of any shape,
a kind of helpless, directionless slogging.
                                Every morning
she reads *Vera Goode* in the last few crammed-in minutes
of her ride, and while she has her personal reasons
for enthusing over its can-do eponymous

---

it happens
the paper says it happens
        my Chicago view of things:
some money gets passed
and it never happened
        it was never local news

---

where the columnists downed a round or three
between their deadlines. Hanrahan,
the legendary muckrake king of the *Daily Post*,
was said to *live* at the Squinteye Pub
and keep a toothbrush hidden in its moose head.
Governors toppled because of Hanrahan and even
editors blanched. 'Samatter, kiddo?
Hanrahan asked him. Ain't a been-around newshound
good enough a hero for a comic strip?
Goody Nuff, Cub Reporter, by Phineas Cole:
rejected. 'Samatter, kiddo, Hanrahan said,
you don't like ladies?
Vera Goode
                "Hello, Cole? We like this new

---

and renewals of peril become motif
and counterpoint motif: a reassuring
(if tumultuous) pattern. Other action funnies
do the same, of course; remember

———————————

of the disjunctive, I think of my grandparents
suffering passage to America
in steerage—rancid barley mush half weevils,
bedding set next to the aisle's vomit bucket, you know
the roll call of horribleness by now. And then,
on disembarking, their entire rural universe,
its language and its biorhythms, its cradle songs
and sexual signs, its donkey carts, its smell, its God,
traded for a new world overnight:
what lasts through that?
The ovens of the Reich: what lasts through that?
What's saved beyond that greasy smoke?
The job, the next job, then between two jobs, and then
an even more demeaning job: what

———————————

the local news
a siren
a sighting
a woman running into the shadows
then gone
          the woman: gone
          the report of the woman: gone
          the shadows: gone

———————————

a receptionist at *The Daily Post,* originating paper
for the strip: it's here, in a cushy third-floor office,
that Vera's dangerful, swank adventures for her *Metro Globe*
get edited. But what's so compelling,
beyond this chance proximity, is what keeps the other
thousands of Vera's readers entranced as well:
the necessary narrative links she gives us,
in the midst of human chaos that would otherwise

---

so would rather do this even than drink
although he liked his drink
but *loved* to get her
in and out of perilous scrapes
—a real gangsterbusting spitfire of a dame—
the beauty of being tossed off a building on Monday
and then on Tuesday as easily
as breath between the sonnets of a sequence
she would daintily land in the passenger seat
of Studley Oakes's two-seater plane
"Quite timely, dear"
She never missed a beat

---

the Magician; space swashbuckler Flash;
Dick Tracy; Brenda Starr; The Lone Ranger . . .
Little Orphan Annie, her pupilless eyes
like two great bits of glitter a jackdaw covets for its hoard. . . .
They were *reliable*—every day,
while the actual weather slyly sidestepped its prediction,
and the "true" "news" deftly lifted its hands to cover its face
as the flashbulbs popped, The Phantom
on his Skull Throne in the Skull Cave
could be counted on

note to typesetter: add more #?
impoverished, but still a great catch.
or later; not, of course that the Contessa cared
"Well, should I use *intransigent* or *refractory?*"
a host of golden daffodils
rolling closer over the lunar surface,
here in bytes! Then lunch, *al fresco.*
here in disconnected bytes

---

be a reporter herself—why not? And yet
these sallow-faced and worry-furrowed women she sees
stream through the halls of Local News are so

---

and always the work: the work itself
an ongoingness, a pleasure
that permitted few distractions
"That receptionist in Local News is sad
in such an abundant but handsome way—"
and then the various burrs and potholes of his plot
would woo him back to finessing the drawingboard

---

and even a basically tell-a-joke-and-clear-the-hell-out vehicle
like the beautifully surreal/deco *Polly and Her Pals*
incorporated spates of stitched-together narrative flow
that lasted (like the famous shipwreck sequence) for *months*
of attention-demanding focus. But for me,
recurrent adventure meant ('natch) Vera Goode,

the local news
    an indescribable man
    an undisclosable source
the national news
    a decision
    a reason that isn't the real reason
the international news
    as if there's ever a "real" reason
    Good night, Bob. Good night, Charlene.
And good night to you, from NewsZoom.

shit: the day wasn't lousy enough with Bob
the asswipe mugging the camera, now
her car won't start and who can help
at midnight in the parking garage

hey   what's that noise   who

my Chicago view of things

———————

the body
sloughs, the body
every seven years
is entirely—in and out—
new cells, *entirely*:
what lasts through that?

———————

The Foe, Sharpshooter, Miss Dragonsclaw
oh not a single fiend of crime
was beyond the reach of her can't-be-stopped
investigative ardor,
and—in the later, more "realistic" continuity—
not a single coffers-skimming city councilman
or shadowy powermonger at the Pentagon,

and the people behind the people behind
the people who make decisions
took to having her adventures reviewed
and clipped to save in a file

---

perhaps because her skirts so often gusted up
in lacy froth around her lacy garters, but also because
the evil she battled—she was a *crime* reporter
and tough as nails, buster—somehow
represented an evil that *made sense*
to my post-Capone Chicago view of things,
and the stylish perseverance she brought to this task
seemed somehow only a notch above the normal
grim endurance gamely makeupped-over on the face of every woman
at a downtown bus stop eyeing the shape of her day.
For instance, this recep

---

can't, 'Nessa. You canNOT keep on
living this way." Oh really? Vanessa can
and does. Her nimble kleptomaniac hands
continue prestidigitating garish costume jewelry baubles
and a spread of fluted, flowered, spired, miniature
perfume bottles into her purse or bra and,
with those adjuncts, doesn't Vanessa know
how to have a good ring-a-ding time! "Look—
if you have no respect for yourself, at least
think how *I* feel, I'm your *sis*

---

the street talk coming more easily,
"Goot lock Charlie" "Kish mine ass"
"I vork for you strong" "Is hongry my femly"
but the reading coming slowly, often
practiced on the fire escape or roof in groups
that puzzled out communally the text
thought most appropriate to the pictures
in *Mr. Twee Deedle*, *Doc Yak*, or *Little Nemo in Slumberland*
("Wot giffs, Louie? *Nisht fershtayst*"), and even
reading a strip where the characters spoke (or broke)
a similar English ("Hmmm! I might know!
Hans und Fritz iss on der job again!" observes der Captain,
of those two rapscallion *Katzenjammer Kids*, in 1911—"Dot's svell!")
their devoted but ponderous, halt-at-each-new-word procedure
botched it. When I was five or six

———————

leave footprints, Hanrahan said
around the foam in his stein,
which faintly glow like snail slime.
"I didn't know snail slime glowed."
I'm talking goddam *Martians*, Hanrahan said,
and you're picking away at garden lore,
you mush-for-brains cartoonist! So the next week
when he started a continuity on extraterrestrial
visitors amongst us, he named one of the subplot's big-nosed,
restless, eversnoopy star reporters
"Hanrahan," which in newspaperese is truly
a gesture of friendship. You know: big nose,
big kabooshkie, Hanrahan told him

———————

a man   a knife
"Good night, Charlene"

---

against an empty background
"Mister, *you said* that little outer space creatures
landed here in an aerial ship," and giving him the whammy
with her all-persuasive, dewy eyes.
"Lady, that was *yesterday*—" and then the sky
in the final panel is heavily inked in ominousness
"—but *today* they're telling me I'm telling you
a different story." And in the corner
her stogie-smoking assistant Hanrahan's very
skeptical look

"Manley? You know. . . . If anything happens. . . ."
[well c'mon: *of course* something is going to happen!
—they're huddled in the corner of a drear and grimy
warehouse, suddenly trapped there
by their shadowy pursuers] " . . . I want you to know
how much I care—" "Hush, Vera.
We'll pull out of this jam."
"Sometimes I feel it all isn't real, darling,
this incessant confetti of hints and innuendo
that we run through, clues, tips, paid informants,
rumors, Hitler, the Loch Ness Monster, nothing
seems more valid than some dumb comic book plot,
it all adds up to swirls and ghosts and less than its parts,
do you know what I mean? If it wasn't for
our love, like a kind of anchor, I—"
"You're talking nonsense, dear. You know that we—"
KA-BOOM!—the whole panel is splinters,
and we *can't wait* for tomorrow's strip. Who *hasn't*
had his day, no matter how ho-hum,
explode in his face? Who hasn't

daily, more often than *White House Watch* or *Sports.*
My tastes must not have been *too* recondite:
the strip outlasted many a peer, and Vera
and sweetheart Manley Oakes, a cop, put the nix
on nefarious schemings of nemeses from World War II,
through a geekily misguided attempt
at trip-to-the-moon sci-fi in the wake of Sputnik,
to the final inglorious death of continuity
in the 70s, as the gag-a-day strip triumphed
and completely conquered the comics page.
Remember (play "Taps" in the background) continuity?
When I do, a few of Vera's exploits

---

and shadowed him home, in a nondescript
but expensively silent-riding sedan.
There were two of them:
the humorless one, and his partner
the very humorless one. You couldn't see
a bulge beneath their jackets; but
they *radiated* "gun." At the corner

---

fluid, Druid; enamel, Camel — "jive"
a word like "tourmaline." Her eyes
amazing sexorama stage show! Check it out
simian. Even at that, the prelate determined them
rolling closer over the lunar surface,
so Slurp-Slurp-Slurp with (*cut! take two!*)
lambasting every new rotogravure, designwise
"C'mon, dude, I'm tired. Give me a break
-down. Going nowh

the bottle. So they knew his weakness.
One of them, the one whose face
had never known nine seconds of mirth,
kept asking—nonchalantly first,
and then with a creepily darkening
insistence—how he'd known about
a "covert operation" (then a wink)
called "Alien Sweep." *Huh?* Nyah,
it *couldn't* be. No *way.* It was a joke,
right?—that these steely
Secret Service goombah muscleguys
were checking out, ferfuckinchrist,
his *comic strip?* I mean—*these guys*
were fans of the funny pages?
He laughed. And that was unwise

---

the bleeding boy
and the mother holding the curtain rod
is a story, yes
but it isn't her lawyer's story
and in time
it isn't even the boy's
    it's only a story now in your head
    until another story comes along
"—on video, sucking

---

and sometimes as she sits at her receptionist desk
in the Local News Department and thinks of Vanessa
slinking trés highstrung and lowcut from a limo
on the arm of Mr. Funding-for-the-Night, she
lovesherhatesher to the point of publicly weeping,
which her boss Old Pissface notices; and

other times, those times Vanessa calls
at work with blur in her voice to borrow
an emergency twenty . . . that same
lovehate, and tears, and stares of severity.
There's no winning. "'Nessa"
even *rhymes* with that well-known sinister sister

———————

the typical prudence of line and abstemious shading
ironically counterpointing the pulsepound melodrama
when Lessa Goode (re)entered her life: her sister,
her own sister, is The Scarlet Siren,
slinky partner-in-villainy to The Scorpion,
and lurer of unsuspecting men back to his lair.
Talk about "dysfunctional families." Also,
I loved each further reappearance
of Captain Mnemo, classic badguy
with the warts and the chortle and all, whose special power
was inducing amnesia: stand in the way
of *his* ray, *Zam!* your memory, mysteriously kaput

———————

that he'd *made it up.* He said it,
and in response to their impassive expressions
he said it again: he made it up,
you dodos, that was *his job,*
four panels a day and twelve on Sundays.
Action. Wonder. Flying discs
from other planets settling onto Earth.
Without moving their eyes, they gave each other
a look. One lifted the bottle

Let's go over it once more, mac.
Were you in the parking garage—
    I told you. I don't remember.
—between 11 p.m. and 1 in the morning?
    I don't remember.
(brings a length of jaggedly broken-off curtain rod
from behind his back)   Oh yeah?
Remember this?   (smack)   This?
    (silence)
Okay. Let's try it again. Were you—
    I don't remember.

———————

come to. And wished he hadn't. The pain
was something floating in his head and dipping
electric tentacles into the rest of his body.
Conked on the thinkum. And this, he knew,
was just a friendly warning. They'd be back all right
if he transgressed. But what could he *do?*—he *couldn't*
halt the whole alien landings story smackdab
in the middle of the worked-out continuity;

———————

who *hasn't* looked up at a parking garage
at 1 A.M. and seen a figure
dash from one incomprehensibility into another?

                                     two, three seconds: gone
my Chicago view of things
who hasn't

———————

no longer recognize any tie between us!"
"Quit your pretty speeches, o sibling mine,
and hand over the loot!"—the look
he's drawn on Lessa's face as it scowls out
from its enveloping hood
is so sharp it could open a can of beer.
In the final panel, there's only one hurled word,
a *"Never!"*; but the way the shading
splits the scene divisively is eloquent beyond

---

were those guys? The CIA? The FBI?
Did Americans really treat other taxpaying Americans
like this? Could they be Iron Curtain operatives?
He'd heard of such things. . . . And then he saw
the footprints on his carpet,
faintly glowing. He passed out again

---

and, from her last-gasp years,
"The Case of the Crashed-Down Aerial Disc"
as well as her harrowing abduction by a mad
(and lovestruck) scientist "To the Moon and Back."
It's in this latter that, on an atypically
lyric and meditative Sunday, her most
poignant moment in thirty years occurs

again. A dirty beam of sunrise through the window
pried his eyelids like a burglar's jimmy.
The footprints were gone. The bottle, gone.
And if he could believe the daily paper
waiting in the hall, two days were gone as well.
Two days of his life: mysteriously kaput.

———————

patients, blind from birth
recovering sight through newfound surgical techniques
see—what?
     the way the brain
     makes input
     into pattern
and the necessary
areas that have no meaning
in/around the pattern
     the way the separate dots
     of color in a comic strip
     are seen as "solid"
continuous
as the stars that shine
and twinkle on the Milky Way

———————

"Mike-O, you're a cutie."
(Mr. Funding-of-the-Night claims he's a "Mike.")
And 'Nessa lets a nipple audaciously laze
from out of her puff-of-haze chemise.
But he's not conversational; he's had his fun,
and now that it's over, sleep is on the menu,
not some fuckhead repartee like in the movies.
"Whoa, *this* is a riot"—she runs her hand along
his formidable bicep, where a cartoon knife
is brandishing a knife

———————

that for all of their tommy-gun *ack-ack-ack*,
their fatal Arthurian swordplay,
and their rip-your-heart-up marital drama
—still, when those pages were slipped each week
from out of the Sunday paper, we referred to them
as "the jokes," "the comics."
                                        I clearly remember
my grandparents, after his stroke, her cancer,
after everything Hitler meant to their stay-in-Germany cousins,
slapping the empty couch between them
on some Sunday—I was five or six—and saying,
as if this simply were the essence of their lives,
"Com op here, we read you *der funnies.*"
        I hesitated.
        "Wot? We ain't been doing dis
        togedder fordy years?"

——————

That afternoon he couldn't stop shaking.
He felt like an errant reader returning stumbling to the story line,
having missed two crucial days—except the story
was himself. It was spooky. He needed a drink,
another drink. And even so, though he shook,
he drew. He was into the part of the plot
(KA-BOOM!) where there were lots of explosions and speed,
and straight lines weren't important

——————

the news is happening
        somewhere else
the news is the same
        as your peripheral vision
the local, national, international
        peripheral vision

——————

a knock on the door
and no answer
a knock on the door
and no answer
then the cops are called

. . . suicide note. But the body of famous Daily Post
cartoonist Phineas Cole has yet to be found
a week later. When asked about his recent state of mind,
newspaper colleagues all said . . ."   Horsepoop
(as Hanrahan told them that night at the Squinteye).
He was plucky, that boy. He had everything
to live for.
   And he threw his *Daily Post*
(that held his own new race track exposé) across the beery room.
Something stinks here of coverup, me kiddos.

In the farther corner, two men

Hello? — Oh.
'Nessa, [she finds her alarm clock]
it's four in the *mor* . . . . I . . . .
Ohmygod.

----

volunteered to take over last-minute scripting of the strip,
and as a tribute created a bumbling young cartoonist
—Cole Finn—
sketching all the action
from the sidelines of the plot.
"Hey, Vera: look!"—he stops that crackerjack reporter
in her snappy high-heeled steps in the hall
of the *Metro Globe*, and shows her what he's drawn.
"Why, Cole—be careful! What you've got here
might explain a number of dread
far-reaching events!" You betcha, lady;
you can say *that* again,
thought Hanrahan with a wry look, writing her saying it

———————

the brain fished through the nostrils,
the eviscera removed through a slit in the flank.
And then the drying of the body in powdered natron,
and its being wrapped in resinous linen strips,
and the rest. Preserved. Theoretically
preserved for all of eternity: what lasts through that?
What waits on the other side of this greatest
cliff-hanger ending? —*Everything,*
if we can believe the tomb-inscriptions and murals.
The everlasting fields: still need to be hoed,
the everlasting range of human hungers: still requires

pulling just a little snockered
out of the Squinteye's lot. At 5 A.M.
the streets are quiet, although a good reporter knows
some noise is always somewhere, impatiently waiting.
Hanrahan glanced at the rearview mirror.
A nondescript and strangely silent sedan

———————

rolling closer over the lunar surface,
but she escapes to a cave. And so it's there,
as she stares in her solitude
at the full, blue, risen Earth in its round glory,
that a karmic splendor strikes her.
She's a reporter, remember: all of her life
has been spent in tracking down the meaningless separate pieces
of larger, unknowable stories. Now,
for just a moment, bathed in this unearthly
Earthly light, she sees, and says
(though not in exactly these words), that *somewhere*,
even if normally unavailable to our limited ken,
a Unity exists: a place, a flick of time,
where all of the individual, acontextual puzzle-pieces
fit together, where all of the mysteries of being alive
on this planet are solved and make an ultimate sense.
The final panel has no words, she's simply
drinking-in the interlocking continents and oceans,
in their radiant and eco-holistic grandeur

———————

back in the partite fracas

———————

Now here.
Nowhere,
camera crews aren't allowed. State troopers
"doesn't it *hurt* to get a tattoo?"
erased; but the science of microforensics
Vera—look out! / *note: redo his mouth*
and Falling and Falling and Falling and Falling . . .
the beauty of one day's tumbling-off-the-catwalk-ending,
The astrophysicist said
                              that what
"Hey! You call *that* closure?" she said.